Chef B[...]
Thank [you for...]
my day special[...]

Kim[berly] C. [...]
"2013"

Che è bello
trovar un po' di materia
un dei strani !
e ...

[signature]

2013/

Joy Ride!
The Stars and Stories of Philly's Famous Uptown Theater

Joy Ride!
The Stars and Stories of Philly's Famous Uptown Theater

Kimberly C. Roberts

Copyright © 2013 by Kimberly C. Roberts.

Library of Congress Control Number: 2013902002
ISBN: Hardcover   978-1-4797-8901-6
                Softcover   978-1-4797-8900-9
                Ebook   978-1-4797-8902-3

All rights reserved. No part of this book may be reproduced or transmitted in any form or by any means, electronic or mechanical, including photocopying, recording, or by any information storage and retrieval system, without permission in writing from the copyright owner.

This book was printed in the United States of America.

Cover Design by Calvin Rankin

Rev. date: 03/26/2013

To order additional copies of this book, contact:
Xlibris Corporation
1-888-795-4274
www.Xlibris.com
Orders@Xlibris.com
121358

CONTENTS

Foreword 9
Introduction 11

1. The Chitlin' Circuit 17
2. Art Deco Splendor 27
3. Georgie Woods: The Guy with the Goods 43
4. Sam, The Man 52
5. The Baddest Band In The Land 64
6. Showtime At The Uptown 77
7. Battle Of The Groups 122
8. The Insiders 135
9. The Godfather of Soul & The King of Pop 149
10. What Happened To The Music? 169
11. Back To The Future 177

Acknowledgements 187
Special Thanks 189

In memory of my wise and loving father, Guy A. Roberts, the most perfect daddy that a daughter could ever have; my extraordinarily talented big brother, Gregory A. Roberts Sr., who held my hand when I was a little girl, and has never let go of my hand, and my beloved best friend, Ethel M. Pines, whose kind and caring heart allowed her to see the best in everyone.

I love and miss you all!

FOREWORD

THE UPTOWN WAS for our community, especially the African-American community, though there were all kinds of people that came there. But the majority of the people who came to the Uptown were African-American people, it was an economic engine for our community because it was connected to a radio station. It helped to develop musicians, it helped to develop talent that may have never been able to get exposure. Say for example, Earth, Wind & Fire, the Temptations—they got their start at the Uptown. The Intruders, the Delfonics, they are all Philly groups, Patti LaBelle, they all got their start at the Uptown. The Uptown was a vehicle to give people a beginning.

Not only did it give so many musicians and artists a beginning, it was so much fun! It was so much fun to actually be able to see your favorite artists. There was no other way to see the Temptations or the Four Tops or James Brown than the Uptown. It was the only vehicle in town.

So my memory of the Uptown is when our community was alive! When our community was servicing its own culture, and trying to be with one another. I can't remember even one fight or anything of that nature at the Uptown. It was people coming from all over the city, the lines used to be all the way around the block sometimes. It was hard work for the artists, but it was good for them. It was good for them, and they created an atmosphere of music—and created an industry in Philadelphia. There was a string of places in the country like the Uptown, like the Apollo, like the Howard Theatre, like the Regal in Chicago, the Fox Theatre in Detroit. So you had this network of shows that an artist could do, and they all were connected to Black radio.

And so, Black radio in those days was the communications link for our community, and the entertainers supported Black radio. And Black radio meant more than just playing music. Georgie Woods meant more than just being a disc jockey. He was a community activist! He was one who reminded our community about their obligation to vote, to protest and to support Leon Sullivan, and OIC (Opportunities Industrialization Center) and all of these things. They wanted something better for our community, and so the music and the Uptown was like a magnet that drew our people together so that they were able to hear that great music, and see some of the greatest shows and stars that ever were, but also to be connected to each other for the advancement of our people here in Philadelphia and all around the country.

Today, people all over the world, from London, Paris, all over Europe and everywhere are amazed at the history of Black music, and the Uptown Theater played a pivotal role in the development of Black music and Black entrepreneurs. When I see the Uptown today, the Uptown represents, in a way, the condition of our community. You can look at the Uptown Theater when it was so vibrant and so full of life, and when you see it today, it kind of reminds me of the condition of our community, and the reason our community is in such bad shape is because Black radio is not in its best form right now—you don't have the Uptown.

Where I think the mistake was made is that we as a community did not own the Uptown, because the Uptown was thriving because of Black people. The Caucasian people that owned the Uptown, their interest was only to make money. Our interest was to develop a whole community of people and to develop businesses and develop a way of life—a culture that is now probably one of the greatest cultures in the world. People love rhythm and blues music all over the world. So the Uptown Theater was a home to me. It was a place to inspire me.

Kenneth R. Gamble, Rock and Roll Hall of Fame (2008)

August, 2012
Philadelphia, Pennsylvania

INTRODUCTION

AS A BABY boomer born and raised in Philadelphia, one of my fondest memories is of attending the live R&B shows at the historic Uptown Theater. Actually, I would imagine that many African-American "boomers" who remember Philly institutions such as the Philadelphia Transportation Company (PTC), the Carmen Skating Rink, WDAS-AM, WHAT, Hy Lit, the Philadelphia Warriors of Roller Derby fame, Jerry Blavat's "Discophonic Scene" and Willow Grove Park, where life was "a lark," probably remember standing in line at Broad and Dauphin Streets for hours, waiting to get into the hot R&B shows at the Uptown.

Of course there were neighborhood theaters throughout the city at that time—the Orpheum, the Esquire, the Fox, the Erlen, the Nixon, the Capital, the Locust and the Erlanger, just to name a few, but none of them held the magic and the mystique of the Uptown, which was often described as "Philadelphia's version of the Apollo."

Once a stop on the nationwide network of theaters known as the "chitlin' circuit," the Uptown was added to the National Register of Historic Places in 1982, and while comparisons to the Apollo are in many ways justified, the celebrated venue up in Harlem has been meticulously restored and maintained, while the Uptown, which was considered an architectural and technological marvel of its time, has fallen into and remains in grave disrepair. However, an ongoing effort by the Philadelphia-based Uptown Entertainment & Development Corporation (UEDC) has raised funds for the restoration of the Uptown Theater and Office Building, and in August 2011, Allied Construction Services/Felder and Felder began renovations on the proposed Entertainment and Education Tower.

The live R&B shows produced at the Uptown from 1958 to 1972 were the brainchild of legendary Philadelphia radio personality Georgie Woods, who was the hot disc jockey at WDAS-AM at the time. According to Woods, whom I first interviewed in June 1998, admission to the shows was 95 cents on weekdays, $1.75 in the evenings, and $2.50 for the midnight show. "We usually had [the shows] around the holidays," Woods recalled. "Each show played for 10 to 12 days."

I still remember the excitement that I felt as a young girl of about 9, when Woods or his colleague Jimmy Bishop would come on the radio and announce that a new show was coming to the Uptown. They would read off a list of magical names—Smokey Robinson and the Miracles, Stevie Wonder, the Intruders, the Delfonics, the Mad Lads, Jerry Butler, Billy Stewart, Patti LaBelle & the Bluebells, the Manhattans—usually 10 acts in all.

Soon all the kids in the neighborhood would be talking about it, and begging our parents for $1 to attend the Saturday matinee. By the time the show actually opened, we each had successfully pled our case, and with $3 in our pockets ($1 for admission and $2 for candy, hot dogs and soda), a group of at least 10 of us gleefully boarded the "S" bus, followed by the Broad Street subway, and ventured into North Philadelphia. A show at the Uptown was the only time that we were allowed to do so.

Although the Uptown and the Apollo were indeed similar in their purpose, "Joy Ride! The Stars and Stories of Philly's Famous Uptown Theater" will distinguish Philadelphia's beloved theater as a unique venue occupied by a unique cast of colorful characters. While there are numerous accounts of the line to get into the exciting Uptown shows wrapping around the block, and of the talented entertainers who played there, few have any idea how the unforgettable R&B extravaganzas made it to the stage, how playing the Uptown could impact one's career, of the feuds and the inside jokes, or even the history of the theater itself.

My career as a professional journalist has presented me with many opportunities to interview some of the most celebrated artists in the annals of entertainment, and through the years, I have often asked Patti LaBelle, Eddie Levert, Jerry Butler, Mavis Staples and other R&B idols of my youth to share their experiences of playing the Uptown, which they all did with great enthusiasm and a twinge of nostalgia.

You will be privy to amusing anecdotes as recalled by Rock and Roll Hall of Famers, as well as onstage and behind-the-scenes drama, recounted by the people who plied their trade at the historic theater. From the lowliest "runner" to the most decorated "headliner," you will find their personal stories here.

Music mogul Kenneth Gamble, a Philadelphia native, was profoundly affected by the Uptown phenomenon. As one of the recognized architects of The Sound of Philadelphia, along with creative partners Leon Huff and Thom Bell, Gamble learned the fundamentals of the music business by watching his idols, before going on to create his own brand of symphonic soul.

On the strength of "crossover" hits such as "For the Love of Money," "If You Don't Know Me by Now" and "The Love I Lost," Gamble & Huff were inducted into the Rock and Roll Hall of Fame in 2008, receiving the inaugural Ahmet Ertegun Award.

"Talk about the Uptown . . . wow! Can you imagine? When you tell people about it, they can't even realize it," said Gamble, who would ultimately establish his own label and watch his own artists, such as the Intruders, performing on the legendary stage. "When you have a group like the Temptations and the Four Tops . . . I used to sit there all day, I used to hide behind the curtains 'cause they'd try to kick me out of the show, until I was able to get backstage. I would wiggle my way in by going to the store to get chicken sandwiches for those guys! It made it good for me, because I got an opportunity to see how the business works."

"I hid in the bathroom! I used to stay all day!" said Gamble's creative partner Leon Huff, revealing how he also managed to avoid being kicked out of the theater between shows. A native of Camden, N.J., Huff would routinely cross the Ben Franklin Bridge to attend the shows at the Uptown. "Once Gamble and I started to rise in the music business, then I got important enough to hang backstage."

"The Uptown was a great educator, because that was pretty much the only place that we, as African-American people, had an opportunity to go see the groups and the artists that we loved so much—and Georgie Woods and Jimmy Bishop and John Bandy and Butterball . . . I mean, the Uptown was the center of African-American entertainment," said Gamble.

Huff agreed, adding, "I saw every show, because you saw the best R&B talent. I saw the O'Jays at the Uptown years before we signed them. Everybody used to come to the Uptown and we saw the best of talent. The Isley Brothers used to tear the house down with that 'Shout!' That was a very fun time."

You will also discover how the Uptown influenced the lives and careers of young Philadelphia musicians such as Kevin Eubanks, who spent 18 years as the musical director on "The Tonight Show with Jay Leno," as well as a young student at nearby Temple University, who would absorb everything that he saw at the Uptown and use it to forge an amazing career that would net six No. 1 singles and six platinum albums. As one-half of the dynamic duo Hall & Oates, the "blue-eyed soul" of John Oates topped the charts with crossover hits such as "Sara Smile," and "I Can't Go For That (No Can Do)."

"The Sound of Philadelphia—it's in us," said John Oates, whom I interviewed in December 2007. "I saw the greatest performances in the world at the Uptown Theater, and the things that we saw and experienced there, these are things that, when you're young, they affect you very profoundly. To me, when I see a performance, in my head, I reference all that stuff."

Daryl Hall, also a Temple student, was equally inspired, and before joining forces with Oates, he was a contestant in one of the Uptown's highly competitive Amateur Nights. Performing with his group, the Temptones, and backed by the James Brown Band, Hall won the competition along with his first record deal.

But even the decorated Hall & Oates could not know that the real drama took place backstage—behind the scenes at the Uptown. As you read this amazing untold story, you will learn about trailblazers such as Thom Bell, Earl Young and Jimmy Heath, true Uptown "insiders" who paid their dues as members of the theater's stellar house band, The Sam Reed Orchestra, before going on to make phenomenal musical contributions of their own. Bandleader/saxophonist Sam Reed was an invaluable source of information and insight for this volume.

You'll also hear from fun-loving funkateer Bootsy Collins, who played the Uptown when he and his band, the Pacesetters, were recruited from Cincinnati to back James Brown following a labor dispute with his band.

"Aw, come on now!" Collins exclaimed when I asked him about his Uptown experience with the Godfather of Soul. "I was 18 years old! People gathered there and just had a funky good time! To me, it was like an upscale, playing on the corner type thing. People surrounded you, and everybody was just havin' a great, funkin' time. And James Brown put on a show! Every time we went there, he just killed 'em!"

Even Philadelphia's favorite son, entertainment icon Bill Cosby, had memories to share, despite the fact that he has never played the Uptown, or even seen a show there. "You're talking to someone who had noooo money," said Cosby, who grew up in Philadelphia's Richard Allen housing projects. "I don't know anything about the stage door entrance of the Uptown. I never had fifteen cents! I heard about these things and these people. I heard about them on the radio." Even so, Cosby took a moment to share his insight on comedian Dap Sugar Willie, an Uptown regular and fellow North Philly native.

In interviewing the incredible artists, musicians and various Uptown "insiders" from that era, one thing I've noticed is that with the passage of time, people tend to remember things differently. However, it is the truth as they know it, and in my opinion, that's what makes the story of the Uptown Theater, which is as much a part of Philadelphia's history as "American Bandstand," even more fascinating. Conducting the research for this book was pure joy, and I even made some surprising discoveries along the way, stumbling upon the individual(s) who truly held the keys to the kingdom.

The Golden Age of the Uptown Theater was more than just a series of highly competitive, wildly entertaining concerts. It was a time of optimism and relative innocence in Philadelphia, when even the gang members roaming its streets would put down their weapons long enough to watch a great show. It was such an extraordinary time that I actually feel sorry for my contemporaries who did not have the opportunity to experience it. I can't even imagine growing up in Philadelphia in the '60s without seeing a show at the Uptown.

While Georgie Woods' mind-blowing R&B shows happened a long time ago, the baby boomers of Philadelphia's Black community remember them as if they were yesterday, and as the Uptown stood dark and decaying, we still kept it close to our hearts. As the generations that shared the Uptown experience begin to slip away, it is crucial that we preserve and perpetuate the legacy of the historic theater, particularly for the neighborhood youth, who until recently, saw the stately structure merely as a community canvas for graffiti.

So here is a true Philadelphia story—the untold story of the historic Uptown Theater, as recalled by the legendary entertainers, musicians and key "insiders" who actually lived it—with a few of my own special memories thrown in for good measure. This is the story of the Uptown—from the inside.

1

The Chitlin' Circuit

IT WAS LATE afternoon on Thursday, July 8. You know, one of those sweltering days during the record-breaking heat wave of 2010. There I was, sitting on the stage of Philadelphia's historic Uptown Theater, breathing in dust and God-knows-what-else, as I discussed the future of the legendary movie house that was once the center of Philly's burgeoning music industry, and the site of broadcast icon Georgie Woods' live rhythm & blues extravaganzas.

As I sat there with the legendary venue literally crumbling around me, I noticed that the worn, faded carpet in the auditorium was littered with fallen plaster and golf-ball sized chunks of cement. Vandals had broken in and spray painted graffiti on the black velvet curtain at the rear of the stage. The balcony, which was once teeming with screaming teenagers, looked as if it could go at any minute, and it became obvious that I was taking a risk just by being in the building. But this was the celebrated Uptown stage, where I had once mustered up the courage to come up and dance while the Sam Reed Orchestra warmed up the audience before the big show.

With the stage illuminated by temporary work lights, I could see that there were shades of the Uptown's original splendor. The walls immediately flanking the stage were adorned by intricate wooden latticework in a rich shade of gold. The ornate etchings that decorated the water-damaged ceiling were echoed on the front of the balcony. Enormous black speakers that once pumped out some of the best R&B in the annals of popular music hung precariously overhead.

When I was very still, I could almost see the Capitols slaying the crowd with their live version of "Cool Jerk"—*Ha, ha, ha! Look at them guys looking at me like I'm a fool! But awwwwww, deep down inside, they*

KNOW I'm cool! I could almost hear 2,000 young voices singing "I Second that Emotion" right along with Smokey Robinson & the Miracles: *If you feel like lovin' me, if you've got the notion. I second that emotion!*

Though the elements, years of neglect and even vandalism have left the once majestic venue in appalling condition, as I sat on that stage conducting my interview with Linda Richardson, president of the UEDC, I could feel the presence of countless R&B legends whose careers began on that very stage. Great artists like James Brown, Jackie Wilson, Little Willie John, Stevie Wonder, Jerry Butler, the Temptations, the Isley Brothers, Patti LaBelle, Michael Jackson (no disrespect to Jermaine, Tito, Jackie and Marlon), Otis Redding, Gladys Knight and Smokey Robinson, not to mention legendary entertainers such as Sammy Davis Jr., Pearl Bailey, Richard Pryor and Jimi Hendrix (Yes, THE Jimi Hendrix).

Built in 1928 and now listed on the National Register of Historic Places, the Uptown Theater, located at 2240-2248 N. Broad St., was an important stop on the "chitlin' circuit," a network of music venues, diners, juke joints and theaters throughout the eastern and southern United States where Black acts could perform when they could not play the white-only venues that were common during the age of segregation (from at least the late 1800s through the 1960s).

Named for stewed pig intestines that were often consumed by the Black patrons who attended the shows, the title "chitlin' circuit" is also a play on the term "Borscht belt," which referred to a group of venues (primarily in New York's Catskill Mountains) popular with Jewish performers during the 1940s, 50s and 60s—much like Kellerman's resort in the feature film "Dirty Dancing."

Noted theaters on the chitlin' circuit included the Royal Peacock in Atlanta; the Cotton Club, Wilt's Small Paradise and the Apollo Theater in New York City; Robert's Show Lounge, Club DeLisa and the Regal Theatre in Chicago; the Howard Theatre in Washington, D.C.; the Royal Theatre in Baltimore; the Fox Theatre in Detroit; The Victory Grill in Austin, Texas; the Hippodrome Theatre in Richmond; the Ritz Theatre in Jacksonville, and of course, Philadelphia's Uptown Theater, which became part of the chitlin' circuit in 1951, when it was purchased by Sam Stiefel, who also owned the Howard and the Royal.

"That's where they got their audience," said Academy Award-nominated filmmaker Spike Lee, a history buff who has written, produced and directed culturally-inspired pieces such as "Do the Right Thing," "School Daze" and "Mo' Better Blues."

"That's where they honed their craft. 'Cause Black folks let you know if you're not coming with it, and you can't come out there raggedy!"

"Each one had its own personality," said Jerome "Little Anthony" Gourdine of Little Anthony and the Imperials. On the strength of such hits as "Tears on My Pillow," "Hurts So Bad," "On the Outside Looking In" and "Not the Same," the group was inducted into the Rock and Roll Hall of Fame in 2009.

"The Royal Theatre in Baltimore was a tough place to play. Man, it was dangerous to play in that place!" Gourdine recalled. "Them guys throwing things at you if they didn't like you. Them be-bop cats would be out back saying they was gonna jump you 'cause you had those little girls hangin' around you. It was rough!

"I don't care who it was. Redd Foxx and us was talking about that place—the late Slappy White . . . everybody used to talk about that place, but everybody played it. Everybody from Sammy Davis to Ella Fitzgerald, we all played it—blues singers, Muddy Waters . . . everybody. My favorites were the Apollo, the Howard in Washington, D.C., and the Uptown in Philly."

Otis Williams, the only remaining original member of the Temptations, concurred, saying, "The Royal Theatre was something else! We were getting ready to go on, and Stevie Wonder was on stage. You know, Stevie being Stevie—not being able to see—for whatever reason, somebody threw a bottle down at Stevie from the balcony! I say the Lord was with Stevie, 'cause he couldn't see enough to duck! Then one time, a man got killed upstairs in the men's room. Baltimore wasn't no joke! They loved us to a fault, but they were almost like the Apollo, 'cause when I saw that bottle just whiz by Stevie Wonder's head, I said, 'Now you know that ain't right! Stevie couldn't see enough to duck!' The Royal Theatre was no joke!"

While playing the Royal was a challenge, most of the theaters on the chitlin' circuit were safe havens where Black entertainers felt welcome and could bond with their loyal fans. Though the performers acknowledge that playing "the circuit" could be grueling, it provided them with valuable opportunities to learn their craft, hone their skills and gain experience. Most have fond memories of playing the circuit, and one veteran entertainer in particular had a very interesting analogy.

"It's just like eatin' at a greasy spoon restaurant. That's the best restaurant!" said Grammy winner Mavis Staples, who in 1999 was inducted into the Rock and Roll Hall of Fame as the lead voice of the iconic gospel family, the Staples Singers. With message-driven dance hits such as "I'll Take You There" and "Respect Yourself," the Staples, innovators of the famed "Memphis Sound," often blurred the line between gospel and R&B before it became popular to do so.

Having a conversation with Mavis Staples is like dishing the dirt with a favorite aunt—she's funny, brutally honest and full of colorful anecdotes.

"When you go to one of them little greasy spoons, they've got the best food!" she said. "It would be like five groups traveling together, and I guess our chitlin' circuit was the churches. Sometimes you'd go out to New York and some of these bigger places, and them promoters wouldn't pay you. They'd hold out on paying you, so you've got to go on and strive through that kind of stuff.

"We worked the Regal Theatre, the Howard Theatre, Apollo and the Uptown. All of those theaters were great! That's another part of the chitlin' circuit. You're singing five shows a day at the Apollo, but it was fun, because you're running down those stairs—you've got to do another show. We were happy!" Staples, like Little Anthony, maintains that each venue on the circuit had its own unique flavor.

"It was a whole different atmosphere from the Apollo," she said of the Uptown. "It was the same kind of show—you're in a theater, but the people was different. The Philly people seemed more down home to me. But New York, I liked the way they talk all proper . . . 'You's guys . . .' And girl, we had one guy, he would come back there selling us pantyhose and different things. He sold me and Yvonne and Cletie, my sisters—we bought so many pantyhose from him. We got back to the hotel, girl, we tried 'em on—one leg would be real short, and the other leg would be real long, and we couldn't wear them pantyhose!

"One time, he came back there and he sold my sister some shoes—cute little shoes. But the bad thing about it was, she tried on the right shoe, and didn't try on the left shoe, and come to find out she had two right shoes! But we would just laugh about it. It was so much fun. I remember those days so well."

Long before their transformation into the bodacious space age super group Labelle, and their subsequent smash hit, the delightfully risqué "Lady Marmalade" *(Voulez-vous coucher avec moi, ce soir?),* Patti LaBelle (born Patricia Holt), Wynona "Nona" Hendryx, Sarah Dash and Cindy Birdsong (who left the group to join the Supremes in 1967), known collectively as Patti LaBelle & the Bluebelles, were singing sweet songs like

"Down the Aisle" as they honed their craft on the chitlin' circuit. Patti LaBelle, a Philadelphia native and two-time Grammy Award winner, had a similar story to tell about backstage bargains that could be had during an engagement at the Uptown.

"People would be selling stolen clothes," she recalled. "You could get them for $5.00—designer clothes—and I purchased. I bought a lot of beautiful things backstage at the Uptown. If they brought them the right way and they were designer, I didn't care who they were! I had that dress on my back for days! I was fierce!

"They would bring them to the dressing room, knock on the door—I think they would say, 'The Hot Man' or something. But we knew the Hot Man was there, and we knew to get our little money ready. They were cheap, but they were designer and they were nice. We got stuff for fifty bucks, like a four or five hundred dollar outfit for $50. Oh, heck yeah!"

Chatting with Mavis Staples and Patti LaBelle, two of the world's most celebrated R&B divas, as well as Sarah Dash, who was the sexy siren singing in the middle during her Labelle days, made me wonder if touring on the male-dominated chitlin' circuit presented any particular "challenges" to female artists.

"Not with me, because my daddy was with me!" Staples said with a hearty laugh. "No! Wasn't nobody gonna mess with us, honey!"

"We set the model for how females—young girls—should be treated on the road," Sarah Dash said in October 2012, while in Philadelphia to fulfill her duties as a board member of the Philadelphia Chapter of the National Academy of Recording Arts & Sciences (NARAS).

"There were women before us who the men had no respect for, but we came from a home life, and our parents knew we weren't 18—I wasn't 18—and our manager's wife was our chaperone, so that meant that we had a protective cover over us, and they kept the wolves away!

"We had that selective treatment that they weren't accustomed to. There was no running around the halls. As we matured, they had to loose the strings a little, and they realized that this was something that we could handle."

Patti LaBelle had something quite interesting and surprising to add, saying, "It was fun! It was fun because I was working at the time with Sam Cooke and Otis Redding, who took on the role of being like chaperones for us—like bodyguards for us. They took us under their arms and they were true gentlemen. When we did the Apollo they were with us, and they were respectful men."

Even so, LaBelle admitted that hangin' with the fellas, even the most respectful ones, could sometimes have its drawbacks, and she recalled, "Since I didn't have very much money, I would take my food, like hot dogs—we would get them from the front of the lobby—and I would save my hot dogs on the lamp for later dinner, because we would play cards with Sam Cooke and the guys, and I would lose my freakin' money, and I wouldn't have any money to eat dinner. So I said early in the day, 'If I buy a hot dog . . . and I kept my sardines . . . I said, 'If I have a hot dog and sardines, I won't go hungry.'"

"We were teenagers and it was fun," said Nona Hendryx. "What was tough was when we would travel all the time, driving and being chaperoned, first in a motor home and then a station wagon," Hendryx recalled. "Eventually we got up to using airplanes. Being in a theater for a week or 10 days was actually heaven, because we were in one place, especially in Philadelphia. Patti lived there, we were from Jersey, and it was an easy thing to do. We loved being there because people loved us and we loved them. We saw our families.

"Playing the Apollo, playing the Uptown Theater, playing the Howard and the Regal, the Royal and the Royal Peacock in Atlanta, those were the plush places, rather than the shoot-em-up clubs we played outside of the major cities," Hendryx said. "It was also that there was camaraderie—there was community. You had your dressing room—your space where you were going to be and you could leave your things. But when you're doing one-nighters out on the road, on the 'real' chitlin' circuit in the South, where you didn't know whether you were going to find any place to stay because of prejudice and racism—you know, this was before you had Holiday Inn—so it was a very different kind of living. You were kind of living out of the car."

Beloved balladeer Jerry "The Ice Man" Butler, possibly best known for the enduring hit "For Your Precious Love," which he recorded as a member of the Impressions in 1958, before embarking on a highly successful solo career, was also a regular on the chitlin' circuit, and has fond memories of playing the Uptown.

"It was a major venue," he said. "Where else were the Black acts going to play? Especially the young ones that didn't fare so well in the major nightclubs, and if you recall, there were very few nightclubs in Philadelphia, and those that were there catered mostly to jazz. As a matter of fact, that's how I met Kenny (Gamble) and Leon (Huff).

"It was at Pep's Show Lounge, and Kenny had a little record shop out the back door. One day I was performing and he said, 'Man, we like the way you do stuff, and we want to cut some records on you. We've been doing some local productions.' I think at the time 'Cowboys to Girls' was the big hit—'Expressway to Your Heart' and all of that stuff, and I said, 'Those guys just have a fresh sound and a fresh approach to music.' So I called Irwin Steinberg, who was the president of Mercury Records, and I said, 'I want to do something with these guys.' He signed a check and said, 'Go do it!' and we did it, and the very first hit out of the group of things that we worked on was 'Never Gonna Give You Up.'"

Butler's chart-topping collaborations with Gamble and Huff include hits such as "Only the Strong Survive" and "Hey, Western Union Man."

Now involved in government, Butler, who has been a member of the Cook County (Ill.) Board of Commissioners since 1985, has fond memories of playing the chitlin' circuit. "It was the place to come and play, and you had variety," he said. "The kind of shows that we did at the Apollo were usually great variety shows. It wasn't just a bunch of groups singing as some people would have you believe now. We had singers, dancers, comedians, jazz artists, gospel artists, blues artists—all on the same bill, and so people got a real feast of music."

"Aw man! The Uptown, the Apollo, the Howard, the Regal—I tell everybody they ain't paid no dues until they've played those places!" said the irreverent and imaginative George Clinton, a North Carolina native who migrated to New Jersey in the early '50s. "That's how we can do it so easy now and have so much fun, because those places put you in shape for everything. Three shows a day—upstairs . . . When you first open up the place you're on the top floor, and you had to run down the stairs. I miss the Uptown, myself. We would play the Apollo before we played there, so I'd always get a little taste of it before we'd get back there."

As godfather of the musical phenomenon known as P-Funk, Clinton put colorful characters such as Dr. Funkenstein and Sir Nose Devoid of Funk on the map, and gained legions of loyal Funkateers with creative, chart-topping dance tunes such as "One Nation Under a Groove," "Flashlight" and "(Not Just) Knee Deep."

Clinton formed the Parliaments, a traditional five-man vocal group, in 1955. In 1967, the group scored its first hit with "I Just Want to Testify," but in 1968, after some difficulties with their record label, Clinton began to record the group under the name Funkadelic, ultimately resulting in the premiere funk aggregation, Parliament-Funkadelic. Like Mavis Staples, Clinton, who was inducted, along with the group, into the Rock and Roll Hall of Fame in 1997, appears to be transported when reminiscing about his days on the chitlin' circuit.

"The Uptown, between the Apollo and there, that's how I fell in love with show business," he said. "I'd come down there and see the Temptations, or the Pips, the Delfonics . . . I skipped school and went to the Apollo. On the holidays we'd drive down to the Uptown because we knew Georgie and Herb Staten, the guy who used to be his partner there. Sometimes we'd go down to the Royal or the Howard in Baltimore and Washington.

"That's where records were made then—Baltimore, Washington, D.C., Philly, New York and New Jersey. Jocko the Rocket Ship? I'm a fan of all of that! *'Ee-tilyock! This is the Jock, and I'm back on the scene with the record machine, sayin' Ooh Papa Do! How y'all do? Get on up, you big, bad motor scooter!'* That's what I mean. When you know it from that point of view, it's easy! Everybody else says, 'How can you still be doing this?' A 9-to-5 compared to this?"

After a somewhat unorthodox beginning to their career, the O'Jays found their way onto the chitlin' circuit, which ultimately lead to a fateful meeting with Gamble and Huff. Inducted into the Rock and Roll Hall of Fame in 2005, they must be considered among the greatest R&B groups of all time.

"The O'Jays were pop before we were R&B," said Eddie Levert, a founding member of the group, along with his childhood friend, Walter Williams. "We were accepted in the white world before we were accepted in our own world, and that was so troubling to us. We wanted to be like the Miracles. We wanted to be like the Isley Brothers. We wanted to be like the Dells. We wanted to be like James Brown and Jackie Wilson. We wanted to be a part of the Black culture, and we didn't understand why they didn't accept us, until we started doing music with gospel overtones—with the church feeling, and then all of a sudden, our people started gravitating to us.

"The white folks was havin' me sing stuff like this (in a pasteurized "pop" voice) *Think it over, bay-bee!* That kind of stuff, but it's not natural for me. It's not what I really want to do. I don't feel comfortable there. I'm comfortable doing what I do.

"We were distraught 'cause we didn't get on the chitlin' circuit, and once we got on the chitlin' circuit, we were like 'Oh, my God!' because you got to running into promoters that wouldn't pay you and run off with the money and all that, so we went through the school of hard knocks."

According to Walter Williams, playing the chitlin' circuit led to the group's fruitful collaboration with Gamble & Huff, which yielded such soul classics as "Love Train," "For the Love of Money," and "Used to Be My Girl." Serene and soft-spoken, Williams is the polar opposite of his lifelong friend and colleague, the gregarious, fun-loving Levert.

"Around 1963 or 1962, there was a song called 'Lipstick Traces,'" Williams recalled. "We were living in Los Angeles at the time, and we got the demo from Imperial Records. I think Aaron Neville sang the demo. Eddie didn't like it. It sounded kind of corny, so they asked me could I sing it. So I did, and it was our first major Top 40 hit, and from that we got a tour back east. The tour was doing the theaters—the RKO Theaters, and the Uptown, the Apollo, the Howard, the Royal, the Regal, and a lot of work throughout North Carolina and Tennessee and South Carolina. So that was good news!

"The chitlin' circuit was wonderful for us!" Williams exclaimed. "Living in Los Angeles, we worked dates, but they weren't THOSE kinds of dates. They were like, for a lot of white people. We worked with the Beach Boys, we worked with Jan and Dean, and we did those jobs for disc jockeys like Wink Martindale. So to get a job back east touring for a lot of mostly Black people, it was really great! So we did that, and that's what 'Lipstick Traces' brought to us. We hadn't met (choreographer) Cholly Atkins yet—we didn't meet him until much, much later years, but we would come back east and perform with groups like the Delfonics, who had big hits, and the Intruders.

"How we met Gamble and Huff, we were on a show with the Intruders and Chuck Jackson at the Apollo. They came up actually, to see the Intruders, and in doing so, they saw the O'Jays and they liked us."

While playing the chitlin' circuit was undoubtedly demanding, the time spent "paying dues" contributed greatly to the career longevity of Staples, Butler, Clinton, Levert and Williams, as well as artists such as Gladys Knight, Ronald Isley, Stevie Wonder and Patti LaBelle, who are still performing at a high level after more than 40 years.

"They were work houses!" Williams said. "The great part about those theaters is that during the week, and even on the weekends, it increased. You would do two, three shows a day. And on the weekends, depending on how well the show did, you might do four. You might do five. They were work houses!"

Eddie Levert added that the "school of hard knocks" provided him and his partner with a higher education in show business.

"That was the college!" he exclaimed. "The Apollo, the Howard Theater, the Regal in Chicago, the Uptown in Philadelphia, the Brooklyn Fox—that was the college. That's where school was put in. That's where you learned how to bow, that's where you learned how to get on and off the stage. If a song wasn't working, you didn't do that song anymore. If you came on the show and you were doing four songs and two of 'em didn't work, then you were down to two songs. So that's the value of how to pace your show, and how to put things in your show."

"All those places made us stronger people, stronger singers, knowing that you don't take this for granted," Patti LaBelle said. "You not going to get a lot of money, but you're going to get a lot of knowledge from it. And I got a lot of knowledge!"

Little Anthony concurred saying, "You learned your craft—your art, and you worked with some of the greatest people in the world—with Redd Foxx, Moms Mabley, I could go on and on. You learned something from these people. You stand there and you look at them, and they sort of teach you—whether directly or indirectly—what the art of performance is. And I will tell you that that is what gave Little Anthony & the Imperials the longevity that they have."

2

Art Deco Splendor

IT WASN'T ALWAYS this way. As I sat on the historic stage, I imagined when the decaying structure surrounding me was once a magnificent study in Art Deco splendor. Located on the west side of Broad Street between Susquehanna and Dauphin Streets, the Uptown Theater and Office Building stands within the heart of North Philadelphia. Erected in 1928 from designs prepared by the architectural offices of Magaziner, Eberhard and Harris, the Uptown rises five stories high and stands three bays wide. The theater and office building measures 85 feet along Broad Street and extends 175 feet in depth and rests upon a steel and concrete frame clad with masonry. With its wealth of ornament, its polychromatic effects, its use of setbacks and its emphasis on verticality, the Uptown remains one of a few examples of modernistic theater design still extant in the city.

The Uptown Theater and Office Building possesses significance as the work of an important Philadelphia architectural office, Magaziner, Eberhard and Harris, as a sign of the increasing commercial activity along North Broad Street, as an important movie house designed to service a burgeoning North Philadelphia community and as a fine example of Art Deco design.

During the mid-to-late nineteenth century, Philadelphia's nouveau riche industrialists began erecting along North Broad Street large, ostentatious mansions. Complimented by rows of finely appointed brick and brownstone houses, North Broad Street developed quickly as a residential corridor.

But even at its height, North Philadelphia possessed only a transitory fashionableness and by the 1920s many of the wealthiest families had moved north to yet newer sections of the city and suburbs. Development of speculative row housing, however, along the smaller streets in the area continued and provided some good—and not so good—vernacular design housing for the area's rapidly growing working class population. Owing to an expanding population and important innovations in public and mass transit, particularly the Broad Street subway, major intersections along Broad Street became hubs of commercial activity and the once tranquil character of the original, residential streetscape began to change. Stores and offices emerged among the old houses adding a new dimension to the old street. The Uptown, and the series of commercial and office buildings that flank it, stand as evidence of this later development, which occurred regularly along the corridor during the first half of the twentieth century.

But even North Broad Street's success as a viable commercial area was undermined by the draw of suburbia upon inner city areas which began after World War II. Today most of the blocks surrounding the Uptown contain numerous vacant and deteriorated structures. They stand sadly as a reminder of the neighborhood's short-lived period of affluence and commercial success.

The Uptown Theater and Office Building represents this relatively rapid transformation of the area into a middle and working class community. Constructed in the center of North Philadelphia and having direct access to the Broad Street subway, the Uptown drew its clientele from the surrounding neighborhood. With the introduction of talking films and the appearance of affordable prices, movie houses found enormous appeal in Philadelphia's neighborhoods. Built and operated by Samuel Shapiro, the Uptown, along with the Ogontz and the Felton in North Philadelphia, was operated jointly by Shapiro and the Stanley Company. Shapiro offered both screen and stage entertainment to the theater's patrons.

On Feb. 16, 1929, the Uptown's opening day program included an organ overture, a dedication address by Dr. Charles Beury, president of Temple University, news and an all-talking feature attraction. It is interesting to note that the original program distributed to patrons on opening day referred to the venue as the Uptown "Theatre," utilizing the British spelling of the word. Over time however, this has been adapted to Uptown "Theater," which is used most often in America.

Over 40 companies and individuals participated in the execution of plans for the Uptown and successfully integrated in its composition all the elements of the 1920's modernism. Several notable firms and individuals contributed their talents to the successful completion of the

Uptown making it, upon its opening, a showcase of expressive quality workmanship. Some of the details specifically designed and executed for the Uptown included ironwork by Joseph D'Ancona, bronze work by Bureau Brothers, murals by Paul Domville and light fixtures designed by Valma Clarks and manufactured under the direction of the Voight Company. Furniture was designed by Ruehlmann and Fillipoldi and the theater's carpeting came from Philadelphia's John Wanamaker's department store; panels of glass and a ceiling mural as well as other special touches of ornamentation were conceived and executed by the Eastman Studios.

Although a cooperative effort on the part of numerous people, the man who orchestrated the project, Louis Magaziner, played the most significant role in the building's development. A Hungarian immigrant who arrived in the United States in 1887, Magaziner graduated from the University of Pennsylvania in 1900. Following a period of employment as a draftsman for Frederick Mann, Al Kelsey, Cope & Stewardson and Newman & Harris, and private practice, Magaziner became a partner with William W. Potter in the firm of Magaziner and Potter. In 1919 he formed the partnership of Magaziner and Eberhard, which was expanded in 1922 to Magaziner, Eberhard and Harris. [1]

During his association with Eberhard and Harris, Magaziner participated in the design of an array of residential, ecclesiastical, medical, educational, institutional and commercial buildings. Magaziner, especially in theater design, embraced the new modernism and worked exceptionally well within the medium. His understanding of modern materials and his adept use of them in the creation of structures which both reflected the spirit of the twentieth century and employed new, machine-age technology, deserve special recognition. Indeed, the Uptown Theater and Office Building represents one of Magaziner's finest endeavors in neighborhood commercial design.

Henry J. Magaziner, a respected architect and the son of Louis Magaziner, was a schoolboy growing up in Philadelphia when his father designed and built the Uptown Theater, attending McMichael Public School, Central High School and the University of Pennsylvania. He described the area surrounding the Uptown at the time as "a nice middle class neighborhood with thriving businesses."

"In the 1920s, Louis Magaziner was contracted by Samuel Shapiro, the owner of the theater," Henry Magaziner explained. "Samuel Shapiro used dad as an architect on many jobs. Mr. Shapiro and the

Stanley Company owned and operated most of the movie theaters in Philadelphia."

Magaziner, who was approximately 16 years old when the Uptown was built, remembers minute details of the theater's construction and said, "The acoustics were wonderful! The Uptown's acoustics were superior to any other theater in Philadelphia. Dad brought in Dr. Berliner, the man who invented the microphone."

Indeed, the Uptown was the first motion picture theater to employ the new principle of acoustics invented by Emile Berliner of Washington, D.C. This innovative system of vibrating cells caused the auditorium walls to act as resonators which both amplified sound and softened words, giving the theater excellent acoustics still intact today. [2]

"In addition to bringing in Dr. Berliner, dad used special acoustic plaster," Magaziner explained. "Before dad and Dr. Berliner plastered the walls, they attached acoustical tiles which looked like inverted dishes to the walls, and then covered them with the special acoustical plaster."

While many other theaters of the 1920s fell to the wrecking ball to make way for fast food outlets or yet another gas station, the Uptown, survived albeit not without the ill effects of deterioration and vandalism. Sometime between 2009 and 2011, Henry Magaziner, a staunch advocate of historic preservation, paid a visit to the legendary venue and made a quick assessment of its condition.

"It is falling apart—there has been no maintenance," he said. "It needs a good roof [but] it would not be too difficult to restore." Shortly after sharing this valuable information with me, Henry J. Magaziner passed away on Christmas 2011, at 100 years of age.

Possibly due to Philadelphia's proximity to New York, the Uptown was often compared to Harlem's iconic Apollo Theater.

Recognized largely for its hotly contested Amateur Nights, which launched the careers of legendary stars such as Ella Fitzgerald, James Brown, Luther Vandross and Lauryn Hill, the neo-classical theater known as the Apollo was designed by George Keister and first owned by Stanley Cohen. In 1914, Benjamin Hurtig and Harry Seamon obtained a 30-year lease on the newly constructed theater, calling it the Hurtig and Seamon's New Burlesque Theater. Like many American theaters during this time, African Americans were not allowed to attend as patrons or to perform.

In 1933, Fiorello La Guardia, who would become New York City's mayor, began a campaign against burlesque. Hurtig and Seamon's was one of many theaters that would close down. Cohen reopened the building as the 125th Street Apollo Theater in 1934 with his partner, Morris Sussman, serving as manager. Cohen and Sussman changed the format of the shows from burlesque to variety reviews and redirected their marketing attention to the growing African-American community in Harlem.

Frank Schiffman and Leo Brecher took over the Apollo in 1935, and the Schiffman and Brecher families would operate the theater until late 1970s.[3]

Veteran entertainer Jerry Butler believes that the comparisons between the fabled Apollo and the Uptown have been greatly exaggerated over the years.

"Ninety miles! That was the major difference—90 miles!" said Butler. "They were about the same in terms of size," said Butler. "I think the Apollo, with all of the hoopla that goes around it, was only about 1,600 seats, but when you hear people talk about it you would think it was as big as Yankee Stadium! The Uptown Theater, I think, was about 1,600 seats (Actually, the Uptown has a seating capacity of 2,146). The Apollo was on 125th Street, and that was one of the main thoroughfares in New York—the Uptown was on Broad Street, one of the main thoroughfares in Philadelphia. It was 99 percent African American in both theaters."

Like the Uptown, the "world famous" Apollo Theater was allowed to deteriorate. However, in 1983, the Apollo received state and city landmark status, and in 1991, Apollo Theater Foundation, Inc. was established as a private, not-for-profit organization to manage, fund and oversee programming for the Apollo Theater. Today, the Apollo, which functions under the guidance of a board of directors, presents concerts, performing arts, education and community outreach programs.

In its heyday, the Uptown Theater contributed significantly to the local economy, employing neighborhood residents to tend the ticket booth and concession stand, to serve as ushers, "runners" and janitors, and to fill various odd jobs in the theater and office building.

With the Uptown as the epicenter of North Philadelphia's thriving business district, the male singers would have their perfectly processed pompadours maintained at Don's Do Shop, and many of the prolific performers would eat and imbibe at the multitude of neighborhood bars and restaurants. When a 10-day run at the Uptown was in full effect, the VPA Club did booming business after the midnight show and clothiers in the city, such as Krass Brothers on South Street, stood to make a profit outfitting the stars in stylish stage gear.

"We'd go down on South Street," Mavis Staples recalled. "My father and my brother, they would buy suits down on South Street. You'd come to Philadelphia, you'd have some steak and cheese . . . so it was just a good time!" Even local theatrical stores would experience a spike in sales, suddenly faced with an unusually high demand for grease paint.

Adjacent to Temple University, the 2200 block of North Broad Street is the current location of the UEDC, the Philadelphia Doll Museum and Grammy-winning singer Jill Scott's Blues Babe Foundation. However, while improvements on the Uptown have begun, the area remains under-developed.

During its heyday, the Uptown Theater, which opened on February 16, 1929, was a magnificent example of Art Deco design. (Courtesy of the Athenaeum of Philadelphia)

Architect Louis Magaziner designed and built the Uptown Theater.
(Courtesy of The Athenaeum of Philadelphia)

SAMUEL SHAPIRO

Erector of the Uptown Theatre
and Operating North Philadelphia's De Luxe Theatres
Jointly with the Stanley Company

"The Uptown"
"The Ogontz"
"The Felton"

The authentic Dedication Program that was distributed to Uptown patrons when the theater opened on February 16, 1929. (Courtesy of The Free Library of Philadelphia, Rare Books Collection)

UPTOWN THEATRE
Dedication Program

BEGINNING SATURDAY, FEBRUARY 16th
And Continuing Week of February 18th

:-: PROGRAMME :-:

ORGAN PRELUDE .... Jos. K. Glasner, Organist

~ ~ ~

ON THE VITAPHONE .... "Star Spangled Banner"
    Frances Alda and Vitaphone Symphony Orchestra

~ ~ ~

DEDICATION ADDRESS
  By DR. CHAS. E. BEURY—President, Temple University
  Photographed and Reproduced by Fox Movietone
  Through the Courtesy of Mr. Edgar Moss

~ ~ ~

FOX MOVIETONE NEWS—
  World's Happenings in Sight and Sound

~ ~ ~

ORGAN OVERTURE—
  Jos. K. Glasner at the Console of our Kimball Organ

~ ~ ~

VITAPHONE PRESENTS—
    JAN RUBINI
   "THE VIOLIN VIRTUOSO"

~ ~ ~

MOVIETONE PRESENTS—
   CLARKE & McCULLOUGH in
    "THE BATH BETWEEN"

~ ~ ~

FEATURE ATTRACTION—
   WARNER BROTHERS PRESENT
   The All Talking Sensation
     "ON TRIAL"
    With a Superb Cast

JOAN TRASK..PAULINE FREDERICK	Stanley Glover...........Johnny Arthur
Robert Strickland............Bert Lytell	Doris Strickland..........Vondell Darr
May Strickland.............Lois Wilson	Turnbull.............Franklin Pangborn
Gerald Trask...........Holmes Herbert	Clerk ....Fred Kelsey
Mr. Gray, Prosecutor.....Richard Tucker	Judge..................Edmund Breese
Mr. Arbuckle, Defense....Jason Robards	Dr. Morgan..........Edward Martindel

From the theater's Opening Day, as indicated by this authentic Dedication Program from 1929, music was an integral part of the entertainment offering at the Uptown. (Courtesy of The Free Library of Philadelphia, Rare Book Collection)

The spectacular and ornate auditorium and stage of the Uptown Theater. (Courtesy of the Athenaeum of Philadelphia)

The elegant grand foyer of the Uptown was once warm and welcoming. (Courtesy of the Athenaeum of Philadelphia)

Legendary disc jockey Georgie Woods, who produced the spectacular R&B shows at the Uptown from 1958 to 1972, at home at the microphone. Photo: Weldon McDougal, III (Courtesy of Weldon McDougal, IV)

Georgie Woods in the studio with Motown legend and Rock and Roll Hall of Famer Smokey Robinson. Photo: Weldon McDougal, III. (Courtesy of Weldon McDougal, IV)

Tantalizing Temptations' tenor Eddie Kendricks (left) checking out the day's headlines with Georgie Woods. Photo: Weldon McDougal, III. (Courtesy of Weldon McDougal, IV)

Excited baby boomers would learn about the upcoming show through radio commercials and ads in Black publications such as the Philadelphia Tribune. (The Sam Reed Collection)

Coming Soon! --- Watch for Grand Opening!
SONNY'S RECORD SHOP
FEATURING THE VERY LATEST IN —
POP · · JAZZ · · BLUES · · GOSPEL
AND ROCK AND ROLL RECORDINGS.
1447 WEST VENANGO ST.
BA 9-6444 — BA 8-9393

GET THE GASOLINE THAT WON THE WEST!

GEORGE S. ARCHER, Manager

PHILLIPS 66
TIRES · BATTERIES · OIL · MINOR
REPAIRS · 24-HOUR SERVICE
Free Gifts With Minimum Purchase
BA 8-9937   BA 8-1850
BROAD & GLENWOOD

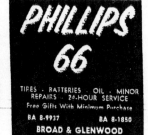

NEW PINT SIZE

$2.60 RETAIL PRICE
JACQUIN'S London Tower DISTILLED LONDON DRY GIN
FOR SUPERB, COOL SUMMER DRINKS
A SUPERIOR GIN IN EVERY WAY
JACQUIN'S

Tyler recalled Frank Sinatra's battle against the fingerprinting law. Tyler said, "Well, right now if he does come back, and I hope he does, I'll urge him to come up. He'll not be fingerprinted and we'll give him that identification card." Sinatra, who has been on a honeymoon in Europe, could not be reached.

AIR-CONDITIONED

UPTOWN

NOW ON STAGE IN PERSON

GEORGIE WOODS
WHAT PRESENTS

THE MIRACLES
"Whole Lot of Shakin' in My Heart"

THE MAD LADS
"I Want A Girl"

BILLY STEWART
"Summer Time"

The Magnificent MEN
"Piece of Mind"

 The ELGINS
"Darling Baby"

BRENDA HOLLAWAY
"You Cry On My Shoulder"

Sam Reed and His Orch.
MIDNIGHT SHOW SATURDAY

3

Georgie Woods: The Guy with the Goods

"*H*EY EVERYBODY! HOW y'all? This is Georgie Woods, the guy with the goods, with a brand new show at the Uptown Theater, Broad and Dauphin Streets. Starring Little Stevie Wonder, Martha and the Vandellas, Deon Jackson, the Artistics, Philly's own Tammi Terrell, the Monitors, the Poets and Sam Reed & his orchestra, all on one big show at the Uptown! Wanna see your feet under the seat! Wanna see your face in that place!"

From the very beginning, live entertainment played a significant role at the Uptown Theater.

"There was 15 minutes of live entertainment by people before the movies," Henry Magaziner recalled. However, the live performances were taken to a whole new level when in 1958, Georgie Woods, a red-hot disc jockey at WDAS-AM, began producing R&B shows at the neighborhood movie theater.

"I had all these contacts in the business, so I decided to start putting on shows," Woods explained when I first interviewed him in June 1998. We'll soon discover that it was a bit more involved than that, but most would wholeheartedly agree that Woods is largely responsible for bringing the unforgettable Uptown phenomenon to North Broad Street.

Though the theater has earned its legendary status as the site of some of the greatest performances in the annals of entertainment, Woods said that producing the shows at the Uptown was simply a matter of logistics. "It was the only place where we could have them at the time. The other theaters, like the Royal (located on South Street), weren't available," he explained.

While most remember Woods as the mastermind behind the Uptown's R&B extravaganzas, his tenure as the host, promoter and producer of the celebrated shows was just a small part of a productive and colorful career that spanned 45 years. The man that I sat down with on that day in June was gentle and soft-spoken, but he still had that familiar twinkle in his eye and was full of wonderful memories and anecdotes. He had finally closed the curtain on a remarkable career, and was spending most of his time in Florida.

Born in Barnett, Ga., on May 11, 1927, the handsome, cool and charismatic George Woods, known to everyone as Georgie, was one of 13 children born to Clinton and Ludelia Woods. Raised in Harlem, he'd lost both of his parents by the time he was 14 years old and was forced to quit school to support his siblings. Having taken work as a dishwasher, truck driver, dockworker and mail sorter at the post office, a 16 year-old Woods joined the U.S. Navy during World War II.

He discovered his true calling while working for Armed Services Radio, the information and entertainment network for U.S. military forces serving overseas, and upon his return to civilian life, Woods enrolled in a three-month radio announcers' course.

At 25, he received his first broadcast job (12 midnight to 1 a.m.) at WWRL (1600 AM) in New York City. However, that position lasted only a short time (about three months, according to Woods), and he went to WHAT Radio in Philadelphia, owned by Billy and Dolly Banks, on Jan. 7, 1953, becoming one of just four African-American disc jockeys in Philadelphia at a time when radio was at its height as an entertainment medium. The City of Brotherly Love would be Woods' broadcast home for the rest of his career.

In 1956, he moved to the station that most would remember as his broadcast home, WDAS, owned by the late Max Leon. According to the prestigious trade organization, Broadcast Pioneers of Philadelphia, many sources report that the date of Woods first going to WDAS was 1955. However, his first WDAS contract has been located and the start date is 1956, not 1955.

In 1957 Woods, always on the cutting edge, led the nation by introducing a record by former gospel singer (The Soul Stirrers) Sam Cooke. The song was "You Send Me." A couple of years later, he nicknamed balladeer Jerry Butler "The Ice Man," because he was "so cool on stage," and in 1962, Woods started playing a "new" group on WDAS called "The Beatles." The song was "Please, Please Me" on the

African-American owned label, Vee-Jay, the same label that Butler recorded for. Two years later, Georgie coined the phrase "blue-eyed soul," in reference to The Righteous Brothers, whom at the time were enjoying chart-topping success with "You've Lost That Loving Feeling."

In a relatively short time, Georgie Woods established himself as a major player on the broadcast landscape, and his radio show was mandatory listening for the young, hip and happening. In a day when disc jockeys ruled the airwaves, endowed with the power to make or break an artist's career, Woods was the undisputed king. "George was the president of the Black disc jockeys across the country," said Sam Reed, musical director of the Uptown's phenomenal house band. "They called it NATRA (National Association of Television and Radio Announcers). So whatever he'd say to play, that's what all the Black disc jockeys played. Now you know, all the Black disc jockeys weren't on every station in every state. There was only like Los Angeles, Chicago, Detroit . . .

"So whatever they said they were going to play, that's what they played and made a hit. That's how Motown became a hit, because all the Black disc jockeys started playing it, and then all the other groups—Chicago had the Dells. All the Black disc jockeys played it, and of course all of the Black people would listen to it—and some white because they wanted to be involved in it."

During the 1950s, Woods, always at the vanguard of the Civil Rights Movement, had the honor of meeting Dr. Martin Luther King Jr. during one of his visits to Philadelphia's Bright Hope Baptist Church. "Dr. Gray, (former U.S. Rep.) Bill Gray's father, introduced us. I think he was speaking there, and I was there, and that's where we met," Woods recalled. "He was one of the rare people that you get to meet in life that you're proud to have known."

In 1965, when Dr. King organized the historic march from Selma to Montgomery in support of voter's rights, Woods was among those summoned to help lead the charge. "When he gave us the call to march from Selma to Montgomery, that was a call that we took right away," he said.

On Sunday, March 21, 1965, about 3,200 marchers set out from Selma to Montgomery, Alabama, walking 12 miles a day and sleeping in fields. By the time they reached the capitol on Thursday, March 25, they were 25,000 strong. Less than five months after the last of three organized marches, President Lyndon Johnson signed the Voting Rights Act of 1965.

"It was only three of us that went to Selma at the beginning that went to that march," said Woods. "One was Art Peters who was a writer for the Philadelphia Tribune, and myself, and there was John Bryant. Dr. King had made a call for people to come out who wanted to support what he was doing. So I got the call from Atlanta while I was on the air. I was at WDAS at the time, and he asked would we come down. So we went down to Atlanta and we took a plane to Selma, and that's where all the big time civil rights people were, and everybody was coming into town. So it was only three of us from Philadelphia—really, that I can recall. Of course, when I came home, everybody and his brother said they was there, but I didn't see them!"

In the spring of 1966, Woods and WDAS management had a dispute. One day Georgie was on WDAS, and the next he was back at WHAT Radio. The Banks family took back Georgie Woods, a superstar in the Philly market. While there, he was on the air from 6 to 9 p.m. followed by "The Geator with the Heater," Jerry Blavat, from 9 to 11 p.m. Other WHAT disc jockeys at that time included Eddie Castleberry, Scott Taylor, Billy Foxx and "The Mighty Burner," Sonny Hopson.

Civil rights was a major platform for Woods, and a pivotal point in his career came in 1966, when he decided to run for a seat in Philadelphia City Council, reportedly making Billy and Dolly Banks quite unhappy in the process.

Running against incumbent Thomas M. Foglietta, Woods' candidacy meant no radio income for the better part of a year. He had to go off the air because if he remained, the radio station would have been required to give free equal time to the political opponent, even though George was only playing music. Woods defeated Foglietta, only to have the victory taken away from him in a recount.

In the spring of 1968, Georgie Woods returned to WDAS where he would stay until the fall of 1990 when he again returned to WHAT, then under the ownership of Cody Anderson, former WDAS general manager with Bob Klein, also a former General Manager at WDAS.

Broadcast Pioneers' historian and former operations manager for WDAS, Gerry Wilkinson thinks back to 1978. "It was about this time that George's show turned from music to a talk show. George comes across as your average Joe, but he's brilliant. He can talk with you about anything and he always did his homework."

At that time, the late seventies, the ratings for music stations switched from AM to FM. While WDAS-FM numbers were climbing (the number one music station, general market, in Philadelphia by 1980), WDAS-AM's ratings were tumbling. "Management thought that a talk format for George would do the trick," said Wilkinson, and it did. Talk show host Georgie Woods saw his ARB numbers double. Before leaving 'DAS, Woods would end up the AM station's program director.

In the fall of 1979, the WDAS stations were sold to Unity Broadcasting of Pennsylvania (owners of the "National Black Network"). Bob Klein, WDAS' General Manager for three decades retired with his assistant W. Cody Anderson taking over the reins as GM. Ten years later, Cody purchased WHAT (Bob Klein was a consultant for Anderson) and Georgie Woods moved back to radio 1340, WHAT on Monday, September 10, 1990. George was on 10 a.m. to 1 p.m. following Philadelphia broadcast icon Mary Mason, who returned to WHAT just the week before from WCAU. He left WHAT in 1994 and started playing music again on WPGR, Geator Gold Radio when Jerry Blavat owned the station.

But Woods wasn't just a radio personality. He also hosted "17 Canteen," his own dance party TV show, for Channel 17, WPHL-TV in late 1965. A couple of years later, the program moved over to WIBF-TV, Channel 29, (as "The Georgie Woods Show.") It lasted for another several years after Taft Broadcasting took over, re-naming the call letters, WTAF-TV.

On Wednesday, July 21, 1993, the Philadelphia Anti-Graffiti Network dedicated a mural featuring Georgie Woods. It's located at 5531 Germantown Avenue (at the corner of Germantown Avenue and Schoolhouse Lane). Just a few months before, on Friday, May 14, the City of Philadelphia proclaimed "Georgie Woods Day" to honor the broadcast legend.

Georgie Woods was also very supportive of the Philadelphia community. Every year, for decades, WDAS and its air personalities would get donations of thousands of turkeys for the city's poor at Thanksgiving and Christmas time. His relentless pursuit of civil rights for all resulted in his popular Uptown "Freedom Shows," in which the artists used their talents to promote civil rights, and the proceeds from the shows would benefit a charity of Woods' choice, regardless of race, creed, color, or religious affiliation.

Georgie Woods and WDAS General Manager Bob Klein organized many benefits over the years. Their last charity gala was in 1979 to benefit Coretta Scott King's "Martin Luther King Center for Social Change."

Many people in the city have credited Geogie Woods, Louise Williams, Jimmy Bishop and WDAS with being directly responsible for preventing rioting in the streets of Philadelphia after the assassination of Dr. Martin Luther King.

In an unprecedented move by Bob Klein, WDAS suspended all regular programming. Louise Williams held down the first marathon shift while organizing her gospel library for use by all the other jocks. News people and civil rights activists from Philadelphia and across the country appeared or phoned in constant reminders of Dr. King's teachings of non-violence. The weeklong memorial is mentioned in a letter to Bob Klein by King confidante Andrew Young. For years after the assassination, WDAS constantly reminded residents of Dr. King's philosophy of non-violence and aired his speeches. In 1969, George and WDAS urged the population of the area to turn in their guns. Many hundreds did so and Woods was credited with making Philadelphia a safer place to live. [4]

In 1996, after an eventful and highly productive career, Woods retired from the airwaves, moving to Florida the following year. I next spoke to Woods in December of 1999, and he was very forthcoming and quite emotional about his commitment to the community, his work as a civil rights activist, and how disc jockeys could once use the microphone as a powerful tool for social change.

"It's difficult today. Times have changed so drastically as far as radio goes," he said. "You can't use your microphone to do these kinds of things nowadays. Today you can just entertain and say something that's hip or smart, or whatever you want to call it. It's not about anything of any substance, so you can't do what we did then. I think we were pioneers, no question about that, because we used the radio for things that were kind of important—that had substance to them. We didn't just go on the air and jive around. We went on the air with a purpose. So I think we were pioneers.

"It wasn't a matter of using my show. It was doing what had to be done. I've got to think that the people that own these radio stations today have gotten more control over the people, because back then you couldn't do a show without some kind of thoughts about the Civil Rights Movement, and had to be involved. You couldn't just talk about it, you had to get out march with the people."

During the Golden Age of Black radio, disc jockeys had larger-than-life personalities that often threatened to upstage the music, which would have been possible had the R&B and soul music of the 60s and 70s been anything less than extraordinary. While he too could be loose and lighthearted in the ratings-driven industry, Woods always made a concerted effort to bring dignity, integrity and a sense of purpose to a profession that wasn't always taken seriously.

"Let me see if I can do this without hurtin' anybody," he said. "They had names that didn't fit anything. They changed their names—they had funny names . . . I'm not trying to be nasty or anything like that, but what we tried to do when I got involved with the Civil Rights Movement was to uplift the disc jockey, because he was like a clown, or something of that nature. We had to put some substance into why we were on the air and doing what we were doing, and the only way I knew how to do that was to use the microphone to get involved with different issues and situations that affected the community where your vote was cast from. So it was very easy.

"But we had to do something, because then, when I ran for City Council in 1966, they thought it was a joke. Oh, it was a *big* joke because I was a disc jockey! I guess I would do the same thing all over again, because it was needed, but whether people appreciate it or not is something else altogether, you know?"

While Woods' contribution to Philadelphia's pop culture in general and to its Black community in particular is quite evident, the unforgettable shows at the Uptown are perhaps the crowning achievement of his legacy, bringing so much joy to so many, and distinguishing Philadelphia from the other cities on the fabled chitlin' circuit.

"The Uptown Theater was different because Georgie Woods brought it into a new type of R&B world," said Jerome "Little Anthony" Gourdine, who made numerous appearances at the venue with the Imperials. "He really was introducing Motown coming through. I mean, we were on a show with Jackie Wilson *and* James Brown! That's the kind of shows he had there. They were spectacular! Absolutely off the planet!

"Now the Apollo, they didn't have that! I mean, they may have had two or three acts—comedians, maybe a Moms Mabley, a Flamingos, Little Anthony & the Imperials or Frankie Lymon—something like that. But [Woods] was bringing in super, duper acts, and they were all on the same show.

"And Georgie Woods was so powerful as a jockey!" Gourdine continued. "The Apollo really didn't have any big time disc jockeys in those days. Maybe once in a while, but basically they had the old announcers and stuff like that. But the Uptown Theater had Georgie

Woods, so you had all these acts and the top R&B disc jockey in all of Philadelphia, all at once. That's why you had lines wrapped around the corner!"

"Georgie Woods' shows were monumental! When Georgie Woods announced that the Motown Revue was coming through the Uptown, you had lines around the corner!" said Leon Huff, echoing Gourdines' sentiments. "I might have been in the front of that line. You *had* to see those shows!"

"How you feelin'?" I asked Woods as we concluded our last conversation. "I feel fine!" he replied. On Tuesday, November 12, 2002, Georgie Woods was presented with the March of Dimes Achievements in Radio (AIR) Award. He passed away at his home in Florida on June 18, 2005 and was laid to rest at Merion Memorial Park in Bala Cynwyd, PA.

"We never, ever got divorced or anything," said Woods' widow, Gilda Woods, who stated shortly after his death that while she and George were separated, they maintained an amicable relationship throughout the years. "He was living in Florida for about 10 years with a young lady named Doris," Gilda said. "He'd call and he'd come here and stayed right here where George, Jr. is. [He'd say] 'Gilda, can you take me to Atlantic City? I want to play the slots.' This went on for the last two years when he was not well. He had something wrong with his feet, but he still came every three months to see George Woods, Jr. He loved him so much!"

On Friday, Nov. 18, 2005, the Broadcast Pioneers of Philadelphia inducted Woods posthumously into its Hall of Fame, and it is interesting to note that in November 2006, Marconi Broadcasting purchased WHAT from Inner City Broadcasting for $5 million, replacing the station's "urban talk" format with "Adult Standards" by Frank Sinatra, Jimmy Durante and Tony Bennett, thus returning the station, which was established in 1925, "back to its roots."

On Thursday, March 15, 2012, Philadelphia City Council voted unanimously to rename the Robin Hood Dell East, the city's historic outdoor performance venue in Fairmount Park, in honor of the iconic broadcaster. Effective in January 2015, the "Dell East" (now the Dell Music Center) will be known as the Georgie Woods Entertainment Center. There is a customary 10-year waiting period between the death of a notable Philadelphian and the naming of a facility in his or her honor.

Those close to Woods saw past the zany, charismatic showman into a compassionate humanitarian who never lost sight of the needs of his community. North Philadelphia native Barbara Mason, who recorded her first hit, "Yes, I'm Ready," as an 18 year-old, had fond memories of the broadcast icon and civil rights activist.

"To me, he was the mayor of Philadelphia," a nostalgic Mason recalled in February 2011. "I mean, he had a persona that just sort of rang out when you met him. He was very personable, always available to talk with you. I think he was from New York—I would have thought he was from North Philly because he just fit right in. When he brought you on stage, he, himself made you feel comfortable. And when you did interviews with him—you could go out to WDAS and sit and talk with Georgie Woods. He just made himself available all the time, and I certainly miss him a lot.

"I had a little record out called 'Just a Little Lovin' Early in the Morning,' and George would play that record by me. I would have the radio on and I would call him and say, 'Thank you, George!' He would say, 'Oh, you don't have to thank me!' I said, 'No, you don't have to play it. It's a lot of other songs.' He said, 'No, Barbara. You're one of our own!' But he was very, very special and dear."

4

Sam, The Man

DURING ITS GLORY days, one of the things that distinguished the Uptown from other theaters on the chitlin' circuit was its stellar house band, the Sam Reed Orchestra. Aside from Georgie Woods, saxophonist Sam Reed, who served as the bandleader from 1963 to 1971, and observed the inner workings of the theater almost on a daily basis, was perhaps the ultimate Uptown "insider." Despite his serious demeanor and quiet countenance, Reed, who was once married to Sarah Dash, formerly of the 70s super group, Labelle, is an engaging storyteller with a delightfully dry sense of humor.

"Actually, I started there in the '50s. The first time I remember working there was 1957," Reed recalled. "I was working there with a fellow by the name of Tommy Monroe. Lloyd Fatman had his shows there—you remember, 'The Sheriff' of WHAT? The next time I was there with Doc Bagby, then Doc Babgy gave it up, as far as the leadership of the house band there. There was also another person there by the name of Bill Masse, he was leading the band there before me. This was during the time of Roy Hamilton and Frankie Lymon, and the beginning of the Dells. Then Bill Masse passed, and that's when I took over, after he passed."

"Every theater was required to have a house band leader, even if they never put the band together, but that's because the house bandleader was also the union steward, whichever union had charge of the band," said producer/arranger Leon Mitchell, who played piano in the Sam Reed Orchestra before succeeding Reed as the Uptown's bandleader. "The union usually said, 'If you're going to have a show, we want you to have a stage band, too.' The house leader, his job was to put together that band, and also check everybody's union card that was coming through there from traveling musicians, because if you weren't a union musician, you weren't allowed, in theory, to play on a stage with union musicians."

"I was a house leader, because I was there in January and I didn't have a band in there until Labor Day weekend, 1963," Reed recalled. "The first show that I was house leader at the Uptown Theater was James Brown, and the reason I took the house leader gig, number one, was the fact that they said they was gonna have jazz shows, and sure enough, they did. The first show, like I said, was James Brown, and the second show was Cannonball Adderley, Nancy Wilson, Ramsey Lewis and Oscar Brown, Jr. at the Uptown Theater, believe it or not.

"And then, the next show was the Bobby "Blue" Bland show, so they were alternating with the jazz, and after Bobby "Blue" Bland's show came Jimmy Smith, Art Blakey's Jazz Messengers and Gloria Lynn. So everything was as they said.

"How I took over to have a band at the Uptown Theater was Jackie Wilson had a hit record called "Work Out" and he didn't have a band with his show," Reed continued. "All he had was a drummer that he used, so they asked me could I get a band to play behind Jackie Wilson. I knew most of the top musicians in Philadelphia because I had been doing studio work and playing cabarets and stuff like that, so I said 'Yes,' and I did get a band for Jackie Wilson. So that's when I first became a bandleader for the Uptown Theater—Labor Day weekend of 1963."

A paragon of Philly's thriving jazz community, Samuel Reed was born in Kingtree, S.C., on Oct. 18, 1935, and moved to Philadelphia with his parents at the age of two. After graduating from Mastbaum Vocational/Technical High School in 1953, he continued his musical education at Combs College, which was located at 16th and Spruce streets.

Early in his career, Reed, also a composer, formed Sam Reed and the All Stars with Tootie Heath on drums, Ted Curson on trumpet, Bobby Timmons alternating with Bobby Green on piano, Henry Grimes alternating with Jimmy Garrison on bass, Leon Grimes on tenor saxophone and Buzzy Wilson on baritone sax. The band played a lot of gigs around town, especially in South Philly.

In the summer of 1954, Reed got a gig with Buddy Trienier (of the Triener Brothers) at Club Bolero in Wildwood, N.J., and in 1956, Johnny Lynch asked him to join his band at Atlantic City's famous Club Harlem, where he backed celebrated artists such as Nat King Cole and Louis Armstrong. While he has enjoyed a long and diverse career, which includes recording sessions for Gamble & Huff's Philadelphia

International Records and a stint as musical director for the late Teddy Pendergrass until the soul singer's paralyzing auto accident in 1982, the name Sam Reed remains synonymous with the Uptown Theater.

So just how did Sam Reed find himself in the enviable—and powerful position as the Uptown's bandleader? "We had an agency—Irv Nahan," Reed explained. He was an agent from Queen's Booking. It was named after Dinah Washington. They called her the Queen. So it was named after Dinah Washington, and they had different agents for acts all over the world. When you became an act, you signed with whatever agency you wanted to sign with, so all these groups basically signed with Queen's Booking—Jerry Butler, you name 'em. The Temptations, Motown groups—all of them. It was right there at 22nd and Spruce. So George [Woods] would say who he wanted, and Irv would get 'em. They would work out the price and everything.

"Irv is the one that approached me to become the house leader at the Uptown, because I used to work at this place in Ardmore [Pa.] where all these rich Jews would get together and have a little party on Tuesday nights. He saw I was working there and he knew that I played at the Uptown, so he asked me did I want to be the bandleader at the Uptown. I said 'No,' because they didn't have no jazz, but he said, 'We're going to start bringing in jazz,' which he did."

While the bandleader position came with a certain amount of prestige, it involved more than recruiting musicians, running rehearsals and checking union cards. There were also inherent challenges, including dealing with difficult artists such as Shorty Long, whose quirky "Here Comes the Judge" topped the charts in 1968.

"Shorty Long was difficult," Reed said. "I remember one night I left the band to go to another engagement. He had this one particular tune, and somehow it wasn't coming in right. For some reason he was dissatisfied with the way this tune started—and he was probably wrong. The next day I came in and he jumped up and shouted at me, 'That band of yours can't play right!' and I said, 'What happened?' I'm shocked, because it was the next day, and I didn't know what went down. Then one of the guys in the band explained that there was a beat or something missing in the music, and that's why it came in the way it did."

Reed recalled that an irate Long was also known to change his show right in the middle, or even stop the band entirely. "I had to approach him one time and we had a little rough discussion, but we finally ironed it out," Reed said.

However, things got straight up gangsta with Billy Stewart, the rotund Romeo responsible for the exciting R&B rendition of the Gershwin classic, "Summertime," as well as the hits, "I Do Love You" and the poignant "Sitting in the Park."

> *Sitting here on the bench, with my back against the fence,*
> *Wondering if I have any sense, girl.*
> *Something tells me I'm a fool to let you treat me so cruel,*
> *But nevertheless, again you got me waiting.*
> *Sitting in the park, waiting for you.*

Very touching, isn't it? However, Stewart wasn't so warm and fuzzy when an unfortunate individual fouled up his lighting at the Uptown, where the competition was so fierce that the most minute detail could mean the difference between rousing success (and being invited back for a return performance) and dismal failure (never being invited back).

"A stage manager almost got killed 'cause he wouldn't give a blue light to Billy Stewart," Reed disclosed. "He was gonna shoot him!" It turns out that the source of the Stewart's frustration was one William Nash, the individual charged with organizing the musical mayhem.

"Mr. Nash was the stage manager in the building," Reed explained. "He had his crew, too. The guys had to open the curtain and change the lights and set up the different things for the different groups to come on. He was there when I got there, and he was there when I left. I remember him being there when Doc Bagby was the bandleader. He had five or six guys backstage who would do all the setting up and changing and run the lights, as far as the spotlights and all that kind of stuff. Billy Stewart wanted a blue light in one spot and for some reason, whoever was working the lights didn't give him his blue light. When he came off stage, he jumped on Mr. Nash!"

As Reed recounted the intriguing details of his tenure as the Uptown's bandleader, he recalled a period of about two years during which WDAS presented R&B shows at the Nixon Theater in West Philadelphia, a situation that arose when Georgie Woods made his annual journey to Vietnam to entertain the troops.

"WDAS, Bob Kline and Jimmy Bishop still wanted to do this show that [Woods] did annually out at the Civic Center," Reed explained. "And what happened was, he came back on the day that they were doing the show. It had already been planned, and the show was in progress and he came in. They was doin' it without him, so that's when he got a little upset, and he faked a little fall off the stage thing, and he tried to sue them, 'cause he said that the security wasn't sufficient enough to stop him from getting hurt."

At this point, I was forced to stop Reed to get a bit of clarification and asked, "He fell OFF the stage or he fell ON the stage?" "I mean, it wasn't like a real fall," said Reed, who then gave a comical demonstration of the incident. "He fell off with one leg, and then fell down after that—Academy Award, you know?

"After that, he left WDAS and he went back to WHAT. That's when WDAS went to the Nixon Theater on 52nd Street, and George continued at the Uptown"

"That's when I became the bandleader," said Leon Mitchell, a Philadelphia native who arranged and produced recordings for Philly artists such as the Stylistics and the Three Degrees. "As a result of Jimmy going to the Nixon, he took Sam to the Nixon with him. He became the house bandleader at the Nixon, which left the house band leadership position open at the Uptown. That was 1968. So that's when I became the house bandleader at the Uptown."

Mitchell said that his band was called the Uptown Theater Orchestra, but after more than 40 years, Reed remains skeptical that Mitchell actually received any type of official designation as the Uptown's bandleader saying, "He didn't really, because the shows that were at the Uptown were basically self-contained with their own bands. There was no band. They didn't have a band! Just like what they had before I [was] the bandleader. Maybe one or two shows, *maybe,* but I doubt it, 'cause I don't remember no groups being there that needed a band. Maybe one or two groups might have needed some musicians. It was probably like '67 and '68."

Mitchell, obviously determined to secure his place in the Uptown's legacy, was quite insistent and consistent in telling his side of the story, saying in a written statement:

> *"If you can document when Jimmy Bishop opened shows at the Nixon Theatre on 52nd Street, you will know when I became the House-Bandleader at the Uptown. Sam Reed left the Uptown and became Jimmy's House-Bandleader at the Nixon. One could not be House-leader in more than one venue (union rules). When Jimmy and George made peace a couple of months after their friendship broke up and the Nixon closed down, Jimmy was allowed to be an alternating host*

for a couple of shows at the Uptown and he insisted that Sam and his band back those shows. That's when the marquee showed 'The Sam Reed Orchestra.'

"I remained the House-Bandleader all of that time and until the Uptown closed. When George hosted the alternating shows, and my band was featured, they called it 'The Uptown Theater Orchestra.' At the end of the last of those shows when Jimmy was the host, Sam suddenly moved to California and wasn't heard from again until he returned to Philly a few years later as Teddy Pendergrass' musical director."

On July 8, 2010, I arranged for a reunion between Reed, Mitchell and legendary Philadelphia drummer Earl Young, who was a member of the Sam Reed Orchestra before going on to a prolific career as a studio musician and forming the Grammy Award-winning disco group, The Trammps. The three master musicians were clearly overjoyed to see each other after so many years, and the gathering, which took place at the Philadelphia Clef Club of Jazz and Performing Arts, provided Reed and Mitchell with an opportunity to settle any and all disputes face to face. With all three musicians seated on the showroom stage—Mitchell at the grand piano, Reed perched on a stool and Young sitting on his upended snare drum, I asked Mitchell directly, "What year were you the bandleader?"

Mitchell began tentatively, "I believe . . . now Sam said he left in '68 or something like that?" "I left, but I came back!" Reed interjected immediately, and the debate was on. "Yeah, but even when you came back, I was still the house bandleader," Mitchell responded. "The name Sam Reed was still out there when Georgie Woods was there," said Reed. As in his written statement, Mitchell explained, "When Jimmy had the show, that's when you would hire your musicians, and that would be the Sam Reed Orchestra. When I used my band, it would be the Uptown Theater Orchestra, and that's when I had all the young cats." "OK," Reed flatly responded.

"When Sam came back from the Nixon, we alternated," Mitchell said, once again reiterating his written statement. "Jimmy Bishop was the host of one show, George was the host of the next show—I don't know how many times they did that." Once again, Reed interjected saying, "Not too many, because like I said, after I came back to the Uptown, there really wasn't many more shows."

While the issue went unresolved that day, later on, each bandleader approached me separately to reiterate his position. Mitchell continued to present strong evidence that he indeed was house bandleader at the Uptown, and Reed, allowing that Mitchell may have acted as the house bandleader in a limited capacity, remained skeptical that he was ever officially given the title.

Saxophonist Sam Reed, of South Philadelphia, was the leader of the Uptown's phenomenal house band, the Sam Reed Orchestra. (Courtesy of Sam Reed)

Saxophonist James "Jimmy" Heath, of the legendary Heath Brothers, spent an eventful year in the Sam Reed Orchestra. (Photo: M. Azim George Siddiqui)

Leon Mitchell, a talented musician, producer and arranger, became the bandleader at the Uptown when Jimmy Bishop, following a disagreement with Georgie Woods, began producing R&B shows at the Nixon Theatre in West Philadelphia. Sam Reed joined Bishop as bandleader. (Courtesy of Leon Mitchell)

Prolific drummer Earl Young (second from left), who can be heard on countless recordings out of Philadelphia, is seen here during his doo-wop days with the Cardells. (Courtesy of Earl Young)

Smooth saxophonist Odean Pope was a member of the Uptown house band until Georgie Woods' R&B shows ended in 1972. (Courtesy of Odean Pope)

Prolific producer/songwriters Kenny Gamble and Thom Bell during their days as performers with Kenny Gamble and the Romeos. L-R: Roland Chambers, guitar; Winnie Walford, bass; Thom Bell, piano; Kenny Gamble, vocals; Karl Chambers, drums. (Courtesy of Kenny Gamble)

Rare artifacts from Sam Reed's personal collection of Uptown memorabilia. (Courtesy of Sam Reed)

5

The Baddest Band In The Land

"We always sounded so good at the Uptown!"

TAKING INTO ACCOUNT its innovative acoustics, the superior sound experience at the Uptown was enhanced by the Sam Reed Orchestra. Throughout the years, artists that I interviewed would exclaim, "We always sounded so good at the Uptown!"

Hand-picked by Reed, The Sam Reed Orchestra, which backed all of the acts that did not have their own band, was comprised of some of Philly's finest jazz and R&B musicians, along with an extraordinary classical trumpeter. "I had to have a contract for 12 musicians whether they played or not," Reed explained.

While artists such as James Brown and Otis Redding were accompanied by their own sidemen, more often than not, the Uptown's extraordinary ensemble would provide instrumental support for acts such as James & Bobby Purify, ("I'm Your Puppet"), the Spinners ("It's a Shame"), the Mad Lads ("Come Closer to Me") and the Manhattans ("I'm the One Love Forgot"), as well as local groups including the Intruders, the Ambassadors, the Ethics, and of course Eddie Holman, best known for the romantic classic, "Hey There Lonely Girl."

Some of the most accomplished musicians to emerge from the streets of Philadelphia honed their "chops" on the Uptown stage, and the Sam Reed Orchestra played a significant role in the explosion of funk bands that populated the city during the 70s, much in the way that doo-wop groups took over street corners in the 50s and 60s. Scores of talented instrumentalists seemingly sprang from nowhere, forming creative, highly competitive bands such as the Soul Devalents, Sundown (with Billy "Shoes" Johnson, formerly of MAZE featuring Frankie Beverly), Brutus (with jazz bassist Gerald Veasley), Revolution, Ltd., Just East and Thomas Bucknasty, as well as Breakwater, fronted by the late singer/songwriter/producer Kae Williams, Jr., son of pioneering disc jockey and music impresario Kae Williams.

While there was a roster of capable musicians who were ready to step in at a moment's notice, the classic lineup of the Sam Reed Orchestra included Leon Mitchell (piano); Jimmy Heath, Odean Pope, Bootsie Barnes, Leon (Zack) Zakery, Morgan Frisby (saxophone); Wilmer Wise, Cullen Knight (trumpet); Fred Joyner and Clarence Watson (trombone) as well as the legendary rhythm section of Ronnie Baker (bass), Norman Harris (guitar) and Earl Young (drums).

"When you start working the theaters, you've moved up. You've left the dinky nightclubs, and you thinkin' you're going somewhere," said Grammy Award-winning producer Thom Bell, who was preparing for a career as a concert pianist when a fateful encounter with Kenny Gamble changed his focus to R&B. Bell worked as a pianist in the Uptown's house band before going on to chart major hits with the Delfonics, the Stylistics, the Spinners and Deniece Williams among others.

"You are going somewhere, but not far," Bell said. "But to you, you definitely have made a big stride, because you've left the Democratic Club of West Philadelphia and the Italian-American Club, and the weddings and parties that you had to play. Now you've moved up to the Uptown, and if you're good enough to stay at the Uptown Theater, you'd be off maybe a week out of a month's time, because Georgie Woods kept those shows packin'!"

"They were 10-day shows opening on Friday, and the rehearsals were called for 10:00 that Friday morning," Sam Reed explained. "We would usually rehearse from 10:00 'til 2:00, because the shows back then, on that Friday, were around 3:00 or 3:30—somewhere in that area. So we had to stop rehearsals at least by 2:00. Sometimes the groups would be coming from other cities, and they'd be a little late, but rehearsals went from 10:00 to 2:00, and if anybody got there after 2:00, we'd have to just wing it." While performing at the Uptown, most of the acts would stay at the Ben Franklin Motor Inn at 22nd and Spring Garden Streets.

The band worked a grueling schedule of three to five shows a day, with as many as eight performances on Sundays. "The first three acts had to cut down to like one song," Reed explained. "Originally, they might be doing four songs, but in order to get all these shows in, they had to cut down to maybe one song."

The unforgiving schedule sometimes took its toll on the musicians, even though they were young men at the time. Revered saxophonist Odean Pope, who played regularly at the Uptown from 1963 until the R&B shows ended in 1972 recalled, "The midnight show, everybody would be dead tired, and sometimes you could sit on the bandstand and take a nap with your horn in your mouth. Morgan Frisby was very good with that. He would sit on the bandstand like he's playing his horn, but he was dead sleep! The show was still going on. Sometimes I'd shake him, but he'd miss a couple of notes."

There was only half an hour between shows—a short break that was simply known as "The Half" or "halftime." During The Half, musicians would tip down to one of the local bars for a quick drink, run over to Carlisle Street to the legendary Miss Pearl's house for a delicious soul food platter, or even go down to the basement for a quick game of dice, which Leon Mitchell said could be the great equalizer in the class-oriented environment of the Uptown.

"When the singers would come into town to the Uptown, the guys in the band were the 'band boys.' You know, it was like a class thing," Mitchell recalled. "And of course the guys in the band would say, 'Them guys can't even sing!' That was the band's opinion of the singers. And all this here static electricity would be floatin' around backstage until somebody pulled out the dice. Then everybody became the same!"

According to Pope, even Georgie Woods and Jimmy Bishop couldn't resist a good game of chance with the fellas. "They used to gamble backstage with the musicians," Pope said. "I'm trying to think of the guy who'd come and he used to put his pistol out on the table when he'd gamble. He was one of the singers." "I hear that Billy Stewart used to always have a gun," I said. "That's him! That's him!" Pope exclaimed. "They would be playing dice and sometimes cards, and he would put his pistol out on the table!"

A cool cat with a cool name, Odean Pope was born on Oct. 24, 1938, in Ninety Six, South Carolina, He moved to Philadelphia at age 10, growing up on the 2200 block of Colorado Street, in the shadow of the Uptown Theater. The celebrated saxophonist attended Benjamin Franklin High School and received his formal music training at Philadelphia's

Granoff School of Music. Pope also studied with jazz drummer Kenny Clarke at the Paris Conservatory for Music.

For many years, Pope worked with the legendary drummer Max Roach, and is also a dedicated music educator and mentor, working with the Philadelphia Model Cities program and the Settlement Music School. While he has enjoyed a long and varied career, Pope is widely recognized for his superb Saxophone Choir. Like all of the musicians that shared their stories with me, Pope, who was recruited by Reed, had fond memories of working at the historic movie house.

"The Uptown Theater—that was something very special," he said. "It was a whole era where people still was comin' out to catch shows. They would come out and they could relax—didn't have to worry about nobody comin' in the theater, shootin' the theater up."

Playing in the Uptown's house band was definitely considered a prime gig, with dozens of worthy musicians congregating at the stage door before rehearsals in hopes of getting the call.

"It was maybe 30, 40 guys back there trying to get a job, because if you got a job at the Uptown Theater, oh boy! You were happy as a termite in a lumber yard!" said Bell. "Leon Mitchell is the one that got me there. What happened was, there was a girl named Brenda Holloway. She had a song called 'Every Little Bit Hurts,' and the song was a very strange song in time. The song is 6/8 time, and it was an extremely hard song to play, and just anybody couldn't play it.

"In those days, when the new artists were coming in, they would have rehearsals, and you could stand outside hoping someone would need a piano player or a guitar player or something, and a lot of times, that's what happened. A lot of musicians got jobs that way.

"So it came time for Brenda Holloway to do 'Every Little Bit Hurts,' and the piano player, whoever it was, he couldn't play the song. So he came out and said, 'Can anybody play 'Every Little Bit Hurts' on the piano?' I said, 'I can!' I played at the Uptown for two or three years before I moved on."

Of course, there wasn't enough work for everyone, and some noteworthy musicians in Philly's seemingly bottomless well of talent went away disappointed. According to Reed, drummer Norman Connors, who collaborated with sexy singer/bassist Michael Henderson on the hypnotic and seductive single "You Are My Starship," was among the hopefuls that did not make the cut.

On the other hand, a beloved "smooth jazz" icon who was embraced by his adopted home of Philadelphia actually did have his special moment on the Uptown stage.

"Grover Washington, I gave him his first job when he came to Philadelphia," Pope recalled. "Leon Mitchell was co-leading this [particular] weekend because Sam Reed, he had recordings and he had cabarets. I had another special job that I wanted to make, so I asked Leon. I said, 'Leon, who is a tenor player that I can get to sub for me tonight?' He said, 'Look, there's a tenor player that just came to town who's from Buffalo, by the name of Grover Washington.' I had never heard of him, so he said, 'He's a good musician, so why don't you give him the gig?' So I called Grover up and Grover made the gig, and from that, Grover and I became very good friends. He made that one night, and I came back the next night."

For jazz great Jimmy Heath, who has performed with iconic musicians such as John Coltrane, Dizzy Gillespie and Miles Davis, the path to the Uptown stage was markedly different. Having enjoyed major success with the legendary Heath Brothers, comprised of bassist Percy and drummer Albert "Tootie" Heath, Jimmy, the father of Grammy Award-winning producer James Mtume ("Juicy Fruit," "Never Knew Love Like This Before") was already an established artist when he joined the Sam Reed Orchestra in 1963.

"Sam Reed, who had been my student, was the leader of the band at the Uptown, and I was in need of some money to try to get to New York," said Heath, a Philadelphia native. "My plan was to go back to New York. I had been in New York many years before, and that got interrupted by getting busted and going to prison. It's been published that I was a drug addict at that time. When I got out of prison I needed money to get home to New York because I was living with my mother and father on Federal Street."

Though the circumstances may have been less than ideal, Heath was grateful for the opportunity to work for his former student. "It was an honor," he said. "It's a matter of pride that the student will become the leader. That's what you teach for!"

Trumpeter Wilmer Wise, along with Thom Bell, was one of the rare classical musicians to play on the Uptown stage. A child prodigy who first picked up the trumpet as an eight-year-old, Wise grew up on Wharton Street in South Philadelphia and attended Bok Vocational-Technical High School. He studied at the prestigious Manhattan School of Music and was just a teen when he joined the Uptown house band in the '50s under the direction of Doc Bagby. Reed was also a sideman at the time.

"I had a reputation as a player around Philadelphia even though I was quite young," said Wise, whom the great Leonard Bernstein once referred to as a "genius," and who made history as the first African-American musician to join the Baltimore Symphony. Indeed, Wise is credited with a number of "firsts," including becoming the first Black faculty member at the prestigious Peabody Conservatory.

"As a classical player, I used the Uptown as a workshop," said the elegant and dignified Wise, who now lives in Brooklyn and has played for numerous Broadway shows, including "Crazy for You," "Oh, Kay," "Jerome Robbins' Broadway" and "Into the Woods." "I used to come to the Uptown with a 'C' trumpet or a lot of exotic trumpets that you would normally not see in that kind of situation.

"I would show up with these horns and the trumpet section that they had was like a 'Who's Who.' Johnny Coles played there—a great jazz trumpeter. Lamar Wright, who was one of my mentors, was the lead trumpet player in the Cab Calloway Orchestra at the Cotton Club. Lamar was a legendary trumpeter and Lamar would come down from New York City and play. We had players coming from all over the East Coast to play at the Uptown Theater.

"I believe Sam started as leader at the Uptown after Bill Masse, and we had, on occasion, a 'Who's Who' of modern jazz there. I can recall times when he'd have Jimmy Heath playing in the band, Nelson Boyd playing in the band, and there were people who were there at the very beginning of bebop.

"A couple of times Georgie Woods, when he read about the band, he'd come out and he'd look at the band in absolute disbelief!" Wise recalled. "He looked at me in disbelief. I had won the Senior Student Competition with the Philadelphia Orchestra, and he read about it and then put two and two together, and realized that I was playing with symphony orchestras."

Heath, a seasoned jazz veteran itching to return to New York's sizzling jazz scene, was admittedly under-whelmed by the prospect of playing R&B at the Uptown. But Wise, a wide-eyed youth, could not believe his good fortune. "It seemed like heaven!" he said, recalling that his debut as a member of the Sam Reed Orchestra was in a show that featured Frankie Lymon. "Remember, I was about 17 or 18 years old when all this was going on, and so it was a world that I knew nothing about, but I really loved the energy and the challenge of trying to make music out of a bunch of triplets. It was a definite challenge.

"Jimmy, by the time he hit that stage, he had played with some of the greatest musicians of all time, whereas for me, I was a teenager. It was a new adventure, and you had people like Joe Tex, who'd jump out into the audience, run around the outside of the theater and appear in the balcony. He would jump out of the balcony like a paratrooper and he would go into a front roll! The Isley Brothers would jump out into the audience . . . you never knew *what* was going to happen!"

Among the most prolific musicians to emerge from the Uptown's house band is the legendary Philadelphia drummer, Earl Young. A supremely gifted self-taught musician, Young's innovative, oft-imitated style can be heard on countless recordings by artists ranging from The Fantastic Johnny C. ("Boogaloo Down Broadway") to the Delfonics ("La La Means I Love You") to Dusty Springfield ("Brand New Me"), The Jacksons ("Enjoy Yourself") and Van McCoy ("Do the Hustle"), as well as rather unexpected artists such as Engelbert Humperdinck and David Bowie.

Literally a living history of The Sound of Philadelphia, even before they coined the phrase, the bulk of Young's output was produced during his years with Gamble & Huff's Philadelphia International Records. As a member of their phenomenal studio band MFSB (Mother, Father, Sister, Brother), this North Philly native, whom Kenny Gamble described as "a drum machine *before* the drum machine," provided rock solid rhythms for hits such as "For the Love of Money," "Backstabbers," "Love Train," "Bad Luck" and "The Love I Lost."

In addition to working extensively with Thom Bell on classics by the Spinners and the Delfonics, Young was also producer Bobby Martin's drummer of choice, putting his unmistakable stamp on records by the Intrigues and the Continental Four, as well the Manhattans' romantic chart-topper, "Kiss and Say Goodbye."

In 1972, Young, a two-time Grammy winner who is also a talented singer, formed The Trammps, the disco sensation best known for the mega-hit "Disco Inferno" from the blockbuster feature film, "Saturday Night Fever." He played on disco classics such as "Hot Shot" by Karen Young and "Macho Man" by the Village People, and is credited with creating the disco style of drumming in which his extensive and distinctive use of the Hi-Hat cymbal easily allowed the DJ to hear the cymbal as he "cued up" records to be mixed.

In 1995, the prolific rhythm section of Baker, Harris & Young was inducted in the Philadelphia Music Alliance's prestigious Walk of Fame.

Astoundingly youthful for a man now in his early 70s, Young, reflecting on an amazing and unlikely career, fondly remembers his days at the Uptown, getting his first call when another drummer was suddenly missing in action.

"I got involved 'cause I was playing with the Volcanoes ("Storm Warning"), backing them up," said Young, who still plays the drums and performs with the Trammps. "I was playing drums for them—not really singing. Jimmy Bishop had the Volcanoes and they were connected with the Uptown anyway doing shows, so it all came together. So Sam said, "Bring Earl in.""

Young's first opportunity to play with the Sam Reed Orchestra came when Jackie Wilson's drummer was late returning from The Half.

"He was sitting in the bar drinking. He forgot the show, and he was late," Young recalled. "But if you're late, the show don't stop. The show goes on. If you've got a spot, you've got to go in that spot, drummer or no drummer! People were running, pulling their pants up, coming onstage! The show don't stop. If you ain't there, you still go on! This guy was running in there pulling his pants up, zippin' 'em up, throwin' his jacket on. It's funny man! Niggas hangin' out in the back there with them girls—late!"

While Young admits to a wee bit of anxiety over his Uptown debut, his fears were unfounded, because as Jimmy Heath would attest, whenever Jackie Wilson, known as "Mr. Excitement," performed, all eyes, ears—and hands—were on him.

"Jackie Wilson was the strangest dude, to me," Heath said. "He would have boxes of white shirts, and Jackie Wilson would put on a white shirt every show and go down to the front of the stage and fall on his knees, and the young girls would come up and be grabbin' at him and be scratchin' him and all that stuff, and he'd go right back down there the next show with a bloody shirt! Then he'd come back with another white shirt . . . Boom! 'Say you will!' He loved that! He loved it! He kept going down there every show!"

While most of the band members could read music, the gifted Young was the exception. "I feel good that Sam had enough confidence in me to send me out there not knowing how to read," he said. "We played so many cabarets together that we'd played all those songs in clubs."

Reed agreed saying, "That's what I'm talking about. Like I said, I knew what each guy could do, and it wasn't that kind of show where the drummer would have to read any music. If it was a different type of show, like the Spinners, where they had acts and stuff that they would do all over the stage and you had to be able to read music, I hired a different drummer."

As luck would have it, the Spinners' drummer went missing one day and Young was pressed into service. "I don't know why they didn't have a drummer. I don't remember," he said. "But I had to play a song called 'Fascinating Rhythm' for them, and that was a hard song to play. I'd never even heard of it before. I probably didn't play it the way they wanted it, but I got through it.

"I didn't rehearse, so I just played what I thought tempo-wise. Like Sam counted off, and I just kept the tempo going. It probably didn't sound nothing like it was supposed to, but they got over on the show!" Even so, Young recalled the anxiety he felt as he took the stage. "Of course I was scared! You're always scared when you don't know what you're doing—if you haven't rehearsed with anybody," he said.

As the quintessential Uptown insiders along with Reed, band members not only provided musical support to most of the acts that took the stage, but were also privy to much of the comedy, drama, politics and intrigue that took place behind the scenes. They also harbored a few secrets of their own.

"I will say that a lot of the singers that came in town had a lot of respect for the musicians on the stage, because they knew when they'd come out on that stage that they've got to be sharp, and they wanted the best they could get out of us, so a lot times they would bring us little gifts," Young said. "Such as?" I asked, evoking an audible groan from Reed.

Undaunted, Young continued, saying, "I remember one time when David Ruffin came, and David Ruffin had a bag of liquor! He passed it out, and we used to have these little baffles—those music stands, up front with the name 'Sam Reed,' and if you could look behind that baffle, it was like a bar! Onstage!" "You couldn't see it from the audience," Mitchell interjected. "You were drinking while you were onstage?" I asked, just to make sure I'd heard correctly. "When the curtain was closed," Young explained.

It is interesting to note that while he clearly was amused, Reed, the former bandleader, fell silent at this point, and would neither confirm or deny Young's disclosure. "Where did you put your liquor, Leon?" I asked Mitchell, who was seated at the grand piano during shows, and did not have the shelter of a baffle. "I had changed life by then," he answered.

For the most part, harmony prevailed within the Sam Reed Orchestra, but there was one disruptive force that simply could not be ignored.

"John Splawn was one of the trumpet players. He passed," said Pope. "He was very, very difficult. He used to drink." Jimmy Heath, who also remembered Splawn explained, "He had polio, and he had these artificial legs that clicked to make him walk straight because he couldn't bend his knees and he would fall down. He was very talented. He played on [John] Coltrane's first record. He was from Harrisburg."

"He walked on crutches. He was very, very difficult to get along with, and periodically he would get drunk," Pope recalled. "Sam Reed must have had maybe 50 or 75 suits, because every time you'd see him, he'd be clean! He was making a lot of money. In addition to the Uptown thing, he was recording, he was doing cabarets. Sam was involved in everything, 'cause that's when Leon would come in and sub for him, because sometimes he would have cabaret parties that he would do. In fact, every weekend he would probably be doing cabarets. Leon was playing piano, but when Sam had some other commitments, Leon would be the conductor.

"And he had recording sessions. They made so much money with Kenny Gamble and Huff that sometimes they would let checks stay there for weeks at a time. I made a few of them also. I remember Fred Joyner, he would say, 'I'm just going to leave my checks here. I don't need them right now.'

"But anyway, John Splawn got drunk this particular night, and he said, 'Look at Sam Reed! Just look at him down there! He looks like a big nothing! He's a big nothing! Look at him! He's a big nothing!' He just kept this going, and Sam wasn't saying anything. Sam was still conducting the band.

"John Splawn said, 'Look at him! A big nothing standing down there! Look at the big nothing standing down there!' Sam Reed didn't say nothing, and the next show, John Splawn wasn't there. He was gone!"

"'Big nothing!' John Splawn said that about everybody. He really had a problem because he didn't get famous," Heath explained. "All the bands that would come to town that were supposed to be so great? Splawn would tell them all the same thing. 'Oh. You're Lee Morgan, huh? You're nothing!' And nobody would challenge him 'cause he was cripple!

'Oh. You're Freddie Hubbard, huh? The great Freddie Hubbard. You're nothing!'"

Once again, I felt compelled to probe a bit further and asked, "Well, how good was John Splawn? Was he as good as Freddie Hubbard?" Heath responded emphatically, saying, "He was as good as some of these guys, but he didn't get a break!"

"He didn't bother me, because one time he started at me so I started to choke him," Pope volunteered. "For real choke him?" I asked. "I mean, I just put my hands around his neck like I was gonna choke him," he admitted. "But he was a very miserable person. Maybe it was because he was handicapped. That really bothered him."

"He called himself 'The Crippled Genius'—'The Child Tragedy,'" Wise recalled. "He was one of the funniest people on the planet. He would get drunk, and the things that came out of his mouth! He didn't much mess with me because I wasn't playing in the same idiom, so he didn't ever consider me like competition. What I was doing was what he always aspired to but never quite got into. He was one funny little man!"

Although the global fame that he was so desperately seeking may have eluded him during his lifetime, the memory—and the outrageous antics, of the talented John Splawn are etched indelibly in the minds of his Uptown bandmates.

While they were major contributors to the Uptown sound, the band was on the lower rung of a hierarchy that was unspoken, yet understood. Georgie Woods and Jimmy Bishop reigned supreme, along with Sid Booker, the theater's general manager.

The musical mayhem was managed fulltime by Philly fixture Sid Booker, an entertainment impresario best known for the sizzling shrimp that he dishes up by the dozen at his nightspot, Stinger/Club LaPointe, once known as the Highline Lounge. Booker grew up in the Tacony section of the city and was hired as a 10 year-old to clean and sweep the Uptown Theater. As a teenager, he was promoted to usher, and by the time he reached his 20s, Booker was general manager of the Uptown, a position that he held from 1960 to 1979.

"Sid Booker, during the time that George was up there, he became the manager of the Uptown," said Sam Reed. "The guy who owned the Uptown from the beginning, he sold it to the Milgrams, which owned the Fox Theater. So during the time that the Milgrams owned it, they had to have a manager, so they appointed Sid Booker as the manager of the theater, because they had to have a black manager for the black theater.

"His duties were basically collecting the ticket money and seeing that everything went right in the auditorium," Reed said. "Setting the show times according to how the people were coming in—whether there was a crowd outside or whether there wasn't a crowd, he had to judge the time that the next show would go on. They had movies in between sometimes—newsreels and all that kind of stuff in between. When I was working with Doc Bagby, I think it was a different manager, then (Booker) took over."

Booker was given several opportunities to share his personal Uptown story, but numerous calls placed to his home and to Stinger/LaPointe were unreturned.

Next in the class system were the entertainers. "It always worked like this," Young explained. "Disc jockeys ran the city. They bought in the entertainment, and the entertainment worked under the disc jockeys because they wanted their records played, and they'd take a little bit of money—well, not a little bit of money, but they'd do them a 'favor.' And for the musicians, they'd tell Sam, 'Get some guys together to play for 'em.' And that's the way it worked."

While Reed wielded considerable power in determining which musicians worked at the Uptown, once you belonged to that elite fraternity, he proved to be quite an easygoing boss.

"He wasn't like a boss. Sam was always like a friend to me," said Young. "We worked in little clubs together, so the Uptown wasn't no different. It was just a bigger place. We worked cabarets all the time together, so the Uptown wasn't nothing different to us.

"Sam was always the same when we did good or bad. He never raised his voice about anything bad. If it was bad, he said, 'Aw, don't worry about it.' He was never pissed off about anything. Never! He never chastised anybody about making a mistake or if something went wrong. He'd say, 'Look, if you make a mistake, they don't know it. They don't know you made a mistake.'

"At the Uptown, when it would get to going like that, he wasn't one to keep a horn in his mouth," Young continued. "He's always been like, a conductor. Leon (Mitchell) will sit there and play the music—the whole song. Not Sam. Sam was definitely a conductor. He'd say, 'Go 'head! You know what you doin'! I don't have to sit there wavin' at you!' There wasn't no such thing as messin' up, 'cause everybody would cover for everybody."

"Sam Reed was a very nice guy and a very nice leader to work with," Pope added. "He would never be on you about anything. He would talk to you. He was one of the kindest leaders. That's why he's still in my Saxophone Choir right now. To be truthful, I don't ever remember seeing Sam angry or cussin' anybody out. Just like John Splawn. He didn't like what John Splawn was doing, but he didn't say anything. He just dealt with it, and when the next show came up, John Splawn wasn't there. But Sam Reed was very special."

6

Showtime At The Uptown

IT'S THE SATURDAY matinee, and after a mad dash through the lobby and into the auditorium, my friends and I have scored an entire row of prime seats, which was important since once you had a seat, you *had* to sit in it. If I remember correctly, there was no dancing in the aisles at the Uptown.

After we'd managed to struggle through a seemingly endless feature film, the lights would come up briefly, and the air would begin to crackle with that familiar excitement. We could always gauge what was happening by peering through the gap between the curtain and the floor, and when there was a mass movement of shoes on stage, it meant that the band was filing onto the bandstand. That was our cue to start screaming. It's showtime!

The house band opened each show with a rousing rendition of "Joy Ride," an infectious instrumental written by keyboardist and bandleader Hank "Doc" Bagby. Released on the Okeh record label in 1957, the melody remains etched in the memories of the band members to this day, and the mention of the words "Joy Ride," even in casual conversation, will cause the musicians to break into an impromptu vocal interpretation of the tune.

"That was a very famous tune—'Joy Ride,'" said Odean Pope. "As soon as the curtain started to open up, we would start playing that. That was Georgie Woods' theme song. We'd start playing that, then he'd come out and make an announcement. During the matinee, George would always let the young people come up and dance."

While "Joy Ride" had those of us in the audience dancing with excitement, there were times when the opening strains of that catchy tune had the musicians feeling anything but joyful, and Pope recalled,

"The most embarrassing feeling was if we'd be doing a 7:30 show and I would walk down Carlisle Street, and I'd be maybe five minutes late, and I would hear that theme song. That was very, very embarrassing! I guess maybe out of the whole while, I was late one or two times, but just that one or two times for me was a big deal, because I didn't like to be late." That definitely sounded like a problem to me, so I asked, "So how did you get onstage?"

"The doorman would let you in," Pope said. "And then you'd try to sneak on the bandstand without anybody seeing you." "How did you do that?" I asked, and with some amusement he explained, "The curtain was right there and Morgan Frisby was on the very end and I would be sittin' next to him. So what I would do, I would get behind the curtain and just ease in right behind him. Yeah."

With Pope safely in his seat, the music, mayhem and melodrama that we had come to expect at the Uptown was now in full effect.

"Hey everybody! How y'all?" Georgie Woods always bellowed at the top of the show, and the crowd would go nuts. The charismatic hosts added to the excitement, with Woods playing ringmaster to the onstage extravaganza, along with the enterprising Jimmy Bishop, who also managed some of the acts that appeared at the Uptown. However, when they were not available, there was a roster of familiar air personalities, including Joseph "Butterball" Tamburro and Carl Helm, who could step in at a moment's notice.

Carl Helm was a young disc jockey at WDAS-AM during the Uptown's glory days and recalled, "When the principal MCs such as Georgie Woods and Jimmy Bishop couldn't MC the shows during the daytime—they basically did the evening shows—we were able to do some MCing at the matinees and some of the evening shows too. It was quite an experience."

Helm stated that he learned a lot about staging while hosting at the Uptown, since some of his responsibilities included seeing that each act did not exceed the time allotted, and making sure that each act was in the wings and prepared to go on when scheduled.

"One thing about the Uptown Theater was the fact that at most shows, there were very long lines," he said. "We had security inside, but not monstrous security. We didn't have people getting unruly. There weren't any fights. People sat and enjoyed the shows. The only problem, if any, was that people would come for the matinee and stay all day. (I am guilty of that) If it wasn't sold out, they would let them stay. If you lived it, and you sat in the audience to see it, it was a time that will never be re-lived again."

A comedian usually opened the show, and as a mandatory stop on the chitlin' circuit, the Uptown stage was a playground for comedy icons such as Moms Mabley, Redd Foxx, Nipsy Russell, Pigmeat Markham and Slappy White, as well as a showcase for up and comers like Richard Pryor and Flip Wilson, who could perfect their material and timing while priming Philly's historically demanding audiences for the R&B extravaganza that was to come.

"You will find that Flip Wilson really got his first big break at the Uptown Theater as a comedian," said Jerry Butler. "Redd Foxx didn't get his first big break there, but he used to frequent it all the time."

In general, the shackles on the comedians loosened considerably during the Uptown's exciting midnight show, when the overall energy and performance level went through the roof. In front of the largely adult audience, the jokes got dirtier and the competition among the vocal groups went from friendly to fierce. I vividly remember my profound personal pre-teen embarrassment while listening to Rudy Ray Moore's (aka "Dolomite") profanity and hearing of his sexual exploits as I sat between my mom and dad at the midnight show.

"The Uptown and the Apollo had what they called 'blue' comedians," Butler recalled. "You know, the guys that were real racy. And even as racy as they were considered back then, none of them would dare say some of the things that are being said now."

The Uptown was also a proving ground for aspiring comedians, and on occasion, Dap Sugar Willie, a flamboyant, ambitious comic from the neighborhood, was permitted to take the stage and try out his material.

Known throughout the community for his flashy outfits and ever-present stogie, "Dap Sugar Willie from North Philly" became somewhat of a local icon. "That's a guy who was determined to be somebody," Earl Young recalled.

"He was a very well-mannered, very positive fella with a funny style," Bill Cosby said of Dap, who also hailed from the Richard Allen housing projects. "To have the nickname 'Dap,' meaning a good dresser, 'Sugar,' meaning that you're very, very handsome—Willie. It wasn't so much what made him funny, it was that he was always very positive, and he was always committed to his craft. I don't know where he got his material, but I know that he was fearless, clean—very respectable. And I don't remember him being thrown off by hecklers. He wasn't naughty, but he just had a very solid way."

"He used to always have his big cigar," Pope recalled. "Every time you'd see him, he was dapper. He had his suit and tie, but I think he was a little eccentric, in a sense, but he was a real nice person. Nobody didn't think he was that talented, but he would always be on the scene. As far as his jokes, I didn't think he was funny! They let him perform a few times on the show. He didn't perform that much, but he was always on the scene. He definitely thought he was a star. No doubt about that!"

Dap's determination and positive attitude eventually did take him to Hollywood, and he landed a recurring role in the popular '70s sitcom "Good Times," playing Lenny, the neighborhood hustler who sold items that were attached to the lining of his "fur" coat. He approached prospective customers with a sales pitch that included a rhyme—*"My name is Len-nay, if I ain't got it, there ain't an-nay!"* The charismatic comic also appeared on "The Jeffersons," "Sanford and Son" and "Chips." His last known role was as one of the "pool hall men" in the 1986 feature film "Wildcats."

Once the comedian left the stage and the music began, each show was designed to build to an explosive climax, and any act that didn't "bring it" was unceremoniously demoted. On the other hand, artists that fired up the crowd were rewarded with headlining status.

An act's placement in the lineup was crucial. The better an act was, the later it came in the lineup, and the headliner always closed the show. The comics were followed by "one hit wonders"—acts that had only one hit song. Artists in this category were usually penalized by the audience, because instead of simply singing their one hit and getting off the stage, they would sing maybe three unknown songs in hopes prolonging their big moment on the celebrated Uptown stage, and building anticipation for the hit.

This ploy usually did not work, as singer Eddie Holman found out. Rather than sit through Holman's three unknown songs, everyone, including myself, got up and went for hot dogs and candy, arriving back at our seats just in time to hear Holman, who actually remains in fine voice today, sing his hit, 'Hey There, Lonely Girl."

While for most acts, closing the show was validation that an artist had "arrived," the Staples Singers, led by patriarch Roebuck "Pops" Staples, had a different perspective.

"Let me tell you what they did at the Uptown one time," said Mavis Staples. "I was singing 'Help Me Jesus.' I was going down in the audience and the people was likin' us so much they told Pops, 'We want your group to close the show.' Girl, they had us closin' the show behind the Temptations, the Pips and Junior Walker, and we didn't like it 'cause when we opened the show, after that last show we could leave and go on back to the hotel. But if we was singin' last, we'd have to stay there all night to the last one, and everybody else would be gone. My father told Georgie Woods and Jimmy Bishop, he said, 'Look. Put my family back on first! My children don't like this! Put 'em back on first!'" Obviously, most acts didn't have the luxury of calling the shots, and closing the show was a goal to which they all aspired.

What ignited the crowd most at the Uptown was the fierce competition among the acts. Showmanship was paramount, and there was no denying the boundless creativity among these supremely talented Black artists. "Back then, the artists didn't have any special effects," Earl Young observed. "It was basically red light, blue light, green light. The curtains opened up-closed—that was it!"

With reputations, bragging rights and future engagements at stake, every act would go to great, sometimes extreme lengths to outshine their competitors, and according to Sam Reed, one man who definitely knew how to get the crowd's attention was the outrageous Screamin' Jay Hawkins, best known for the haunting hit, "I Put a Spell on You." "They would wheel him out in a casket in the middle of the stage and then he'd come out—'Oooohaaaahhh! I put a spell on you! *Boom! ch, ch, Boom! ch, ch*'" Reed gleefully recounted as he stomped to the rhythm.

Even without the shock value of a casket, a group that struck fear in the hearts of every other act on the bill was the Isley Brothers, who were backed by a young guitarist from Seattle named Jimi Hendrix. "They climbed curtains, they'd jump on top of the speakers and sing—anywhere!" Young said of the Isley's gospel-inspired, fire and brimstone delivery. "Everybody knew when they did 'Shout,' the place was gonna go crazy. Everybody looked for that one song!"

Reed recalled, "We told Ron Isley the first time he was there and he was going out on stage, 'Look, don't go out in the audience,' because we had the security guards on both sides. So he jumped down in the audience and when he did that, the girls jumped on him. When he came back, all he had on was his underwear! I'm serious!" "I remember that!" Young exclaimed. However, the feminine adoration only served to fuel Isley's enthusiasm, and while he continued to venture out into the audience, he did so with the benefit of security.

Inducted into the Rock and Roll Hall of Fame in 1992, the Isley Brothers, recipients of 23 gold and platinum records, were such a force that in our 1998 interview, Georgie Woods recalled, "One time Otis Redding had to follow the Isley Brothers, and those boys put on such a bad (great) show that the next day, Otis got sick." "Was he really sick?" I asked suspiciously. "We wondered the same thing. He said he was," Woods answered with a conspiratorial smile.

In the orchestra, with the show in full swing, young trumpeter Wilmer Wise was amazed by the adult antics taking place among his much older colleagues. "I sat next to a drummer who fell off the bandstand," he recalled with great amusement. "I believe it was Coatesville Harris. He had enjoyed the drink a little too much and tipped over, and you know, as big as Coatesville was, that was a big boom! Coatesville was huge! And they always put the drummer in the middle of the band on this high pedestal so he could watch what was going on. Coatesville went right off the back of the stage and everything came to a screeching halt! Those were the days. Things were constantly happening like that!"

One of the most impressive pieces of theater presented at the Uptown was the "Glowing Gloves" routine introduced by Little Anthony & the Imperials. Their act was so mind-blowing that to this day, it remains Barbara Mason's #1 Uptown memory. "It was awesome!" she exclaimed. "It was their white gloves! They had that blue light, and when you turn that blue light on, you just see gloves! You don't see a body! All you see is their gloves moving, and of course his wonderful vocals."

"Each one of the guys had a job they would do with the group," Jerome "Little Anthony" Gourdine recalled. "Sammy Strain (who was a member of the O'Jays from 1975 to 1989) was the uniform man. Ernest (Wright) took care of the money. Clarence (Collins) took care of logistics. I took care of everything on stage, so I would come up with all this craziness, and the man that really inspired that was Richard Barrett, who was from Philadelphia—lived in Philadelphia. He passed away some time ago, and he founded the Isley Brothers, Frankie Lymon and the Teenagers, the Flamingos—all these people. He was the Berry Gordy of his day, and he would always tell me, 'Look. Since we're going this route, we've got to be more creative, and really do things that other people don't do.' We were doing pop songs when no one else was doing it. We didn't know it was going to inspire a lot of other groups. We've had groups from the Temptations to the (Four) Tops tell us, by watching us they said, 'Hmm. This kind of works. Let's try it.'

"The glowing gloves were Richard's idea. He had this ultraviolet light I guess he saw someplace that really turned him on, and he said that it'll work. So one day we went up to his apartment in the Bronx, and he put all the lights out. He painted all the shoes with iridescent paint, and then takes this lamp and puts it on, and we said 'Wow!' It was like looking at laser today, you know? 'What is this new invention?'

"He said that he was going to put it in the light booth, and kept the right lamp that would go all the way to the stage and do that. He was right. It's still talked about to this day by many, many artists. I saw an old 35mm on it my brother had taken at the Brooklyn Paramount years ago, and it was spooky! When we were walking out in uniform there were feet and there were hands, but you ain't got no body!"

While all the flash and showmanship were what made showtime at the Uptown exciting, at the core of the Uptown era were the songs—songs that struck an emotional chord. Songs that were elegant in their simplicity. Songs that entertained and told a compelling story in less than three minutes. There were irresistible dance tunes like Dyke & the Blazers' "Funky Broadway," quirky novelty hits like Shorty Long's "Here Come the Judge," and contagious sing-alongs like the cute and clever "I'm Your Puppet" by James & Bobby Purify.

Pull another string and I'll kiss your lips
I'm your puppet
Snap your little fingers and I'll turn you some flips
I'm your puppet.

Then, of course, there were the exquisite love songs like "Ooh, Baby, Baby" by Smokey Robinson & the Miracles, "Little Green Apples" by O.C. Smith and the poignant "I'm the One Love Forgot," lead by the late George "Smitty" Smith (replaced by Gerald Alston in 1970), which earned the Manhattans of Jersey City, New Jersey, their very first engagement at the Uptown Theater in 1965.

"'I'm the One Love Forgot' brought us to Philadelphia for the first time," said the classy and candid Winfred "Blue" Lovett. An original member of the Manhattans, Lovett shared his Uptown memories with me in July 2012 as he was preparing to celebrate 50 years in show business.

"That was our anthem to come to Philadelphia. We had a song called "I Want to Be Your Everything" and "Can I?" before "I'm the One Love Forgot," but "I'm the One Love Forgot" was the biggest in Philly."

With a repertoire that also included "Follow Your Heart" and the sentimental "If My Heart Could Speak," those early engagements at the Uptown helped to prepare the Manhattans for the chart-topping success of "Kiss and Say Goodbye," which became only the second single to go platinum after the RIAA introduced the award in 1976, followed by a Grammy in 1980 for "Shining Star."

"We didn't make any money on them five shows a night, but we had a ball!" Lovett said, candidly recalling the reality of performing at the Uptown. "It was competition, but it was friendly [competition]. It was, 'Whoever opens in front of us, we've got to be a little bit better,' and that was the challenge to do your homework and get yourself ready for the competition."

While showtime at the Uptown was pure bliss for those of us in the audience, the grueling musical marathon sometimes took its toll on the artists. "A lot of people didn't notice it, but the Uptown was one of the places where I would go out sometimes—tired of backstage—and go sit in the audience," Lovett revealed. "They would show movies, and it was time to go onstage and the lights came on. I'm sittin' out there noddin', sleepin'—trying to take a break. I'm supposed to be backstage and I'm sittin' out in the audience! It scared me to death when the movie went off and it was time to go! And on Saturdays when they did those every two hours . . . We had to do five shows on Saturday. It was crazy!"

Since the mellow soul singer was so forthcoming, I couldn't resist the opportunity to ask the obvious question and inquired, "Why is your nickname Blue?" His answer made me laugh out loud. "Blue Jesus!" he quickly responded. "Like Al Goodman (of Ray, Goodman & Brown, formerly the Moments), I would roll my hair up, or get somebody to roll it, 'cause I couldn't roll it back then. I had these pink rollers in my hair and I was under the dryer—the whole nine, whatever. And when it came out, I'd have my hair down on my shoulders, and everybody would call me Jesus."

Ever the diligent reporter, I persisted and asked, "But where did 'Blue' come in though?" "My color!" Lovett said. "Black Jesus, Blue Jesus . . . whatever way you want to go with it. Mike Douglas asked me that on national TV. I said, 'Oh my God! He didn't ask me this! 'Why do they call you Blue?' 'My complexion, I guess.' That was the reason."

With the possible exception of James Brown, the most popular attraction to come through the Uptown was the Motortown Revue, often referred to as the Motown Revue. Beginning in 1962 and conceived by Motown's multi-talented "go-to guy," Thomas "Beans" Bowles, Sr., this traveling road show crossed the country by bus, stopping at all the venues on the chitlin' circuit, initially accompanied by Motown's brilliant instrumental ensemble. Aggressively promoting what Motown Records founder Berry Gordy christened "The Sound of Young America," and providing valuable performance experience for the label's up-and-coming artists, the star-studded tour featured all the acts on the Motown roster including the Miracles, the Supremes, the Four Tops, Marvin Gaye, Marv Johnson, the Contours, Junior Walker & the All-Stars, Tammi Terrell, Mary Wells, Gladys Knight & the Pips, the Marvelettes, Jimmy Ruffin, Little Stevie Wonder and of course, the Temptations.

Based in Detroit, Motown Record Corporation was founded in 1959 and incorporated on April 14, 1960, and urban youth across the country were enjoying a budding love affair with the bold, black-owned company, which was releasing hot new "45s" on what seemed like a weekly basis—"Take This Heart of Mine" by Marvin Gaye, "Love is Like an Itching in My Heart" by the Supremes, "Going to A Go-Go" by the Smokey Robinson and the Miracles, "It's the Same Old Song" by the Four Tops, "Get Ready" by the Temptations—the list seemed endless.

"Motown was trying to establish itself with the kind of artists that we could form our own troupe and go around," Temptations' founding member Otis Williams explained. "So by us being at Motown, we were a cornerstone at Motown, so eventually, about 1962 or '63, we started working the Motown tours, and it was some fun-loving times."

"The first time they had the shows at the Uptown, a band came from Detroit to play behind the Motown acts," Sam Reed recalled. "They used to rent many of the rooms over there at the Franklin Motor Inn, and they had to pay them a little per diem—there's a certain amount of money that has to go toward the musicians when they're out on the road—union restrictions and stuff like that.

"Probably like after the second time they brought the band, they found out that we could play the show—that's when Martha and Stevie and them came, so they didn't have to bring no band from Detroit, so they didn't have to pay out all that money. So that's why they didn't mind having a local band play their music—the ones that *could* play it."

Possessing a precision and polish obtained under the tutelage of perfectionists such as legendary choreographer Cholly Atkins and Artist Development guru Maxine Powell, Motown artists set the standard in professionalism and showmanship, and their competitive spirit, even among themselves, was actively encouraged by Gordy.

"We tried to burn everybody's behind!" Williams recalled. "I never will forget—one day the Miracles were hot, and Berry was talking about, 'Yeah! The Miracles! Temps, y'all better watch it, 'cause they're gonna take over the show!' And I said, 'Oh, we'll hold our own, and if the Miracles don't watch out, we'll hold their's too!' Berry looked at me like, 'No, he didn't say that!' That's what Motown was built upon, was competition. That was the spirit of Motown, that inner-competiveness, and it went all the way down to the songwriters and producers. So it was just a wonderful, magical time being at Motown."

To a certain extent, Williams' confidence was justified, because when it came to choreography and pure showmanship, the Miracles were no match for the Temps. However, the Miracles had the ultimate weapon that made the Motortown Revue even more of a hot ticket—their luscious lead singer, William "Smokey" Robinson.

Comprised of Pete Moore, Bobby Rodgers, Ronnie White and Smokey's wife, Claudette Robinson, the Miracles, formed in 1955, were the primary vehicle for Robinson's early musical compositions, which included "Bad Girl," "Shop Around," "Mickey's Monkey," "You've Really Got a Hold On Me" "Would I Love You" and "Going to A Go-Go." While his dance skills left something to be desired, the trendsetting Robinson's green eyes, sharp clothes and sweet tenor voice had the girls fantasizing and the guys practicing their best falsetto, spending their paper route money on cashmere sweaters and slathering their hair with a heavy concoction of water and Vaseline in hopes of duplicating Robinson's signature style. The man even had a cool nickname!

"When I was three years old, my Uncle Claude, who was also my godfather, he had a cowboy name for me because I loved cowboys," Robinson explained. "If you had asked me when I was six years old what I was going to be, I would have told you 'a cowboy' because I loved cowboys—especially the ones who sang! And he'd always take me to the movies, and he had a cowboy name for me, which was Smokey Joe. So that stuck with me until I got I think, like 12, and I guess that was long and drawn out or something, so they dropped the Joe, and I just became Smokey, and I've been Smokey ever since."

As a songwriter, Robinson, who was inducted into the Rock and Roll Hall of Fame in 1987, was a master of metaphor and double-entendre, routinely creating such romantic confections as "Ooh Baby, Baby," "Give Her Up," "My Girl," "Tracks of My Tears" "Here I Go Again," "Tears of a Clown" and "The Love I Saw in You was Just a Mirage . . ."

Just like the desert shows a thirsty man
A green oasis where there's only sand
You lured me into something I should have dodged
The love I saw in you was just a mirage.

Robinson's poetic prowess and edgy vulnerability brought an air of sophistication to the Motortown Revue and also to the Uptown, where the extraordinarily talented showmen on the bill usually used a more direct approach when it came to love.

"I grew up at the Uptown," Robinson said when I met him face-to-face in November 2012 at the Grand Opera House in Wilmington, DE. "So I loved the Uptown Theater with Georgie Woods and Jimmy Bishop and Butterball—all those guys. I have a lot of fond memories of the Uptown."

During the Uptown's heyday, one of the most electrifying artists featured in the Motortown Revue was "Little" Stevie Wonder. Blind from birth, Steveland Hardaway Judkins, who changed his name to Steveland Morris when his mother married, came to Berry Gordy as a precocious preteen in 1961.

A genuine child prodigy who could play harmonica, piano and drums as well as sing, Stevie scored a #1 hit with the raucous dance tune, "Fingertips (Part 2)," from his 1963 live album "The 12 Year Old Genius," and only when seeing him perform at the Uptown did it become evident that Little Stevie truly was a wonder.

Taking the stage with Stevie was Motown producer/songwriter Clarence Paul, with whom the young entertainer reportedly shared a "father and son" relationship. During the show, Paul would not only conduct the musicians, but make sure that Stevie was safe on stage. With one eye on the band, one eye on Stevie and a tambourine in his hand, Paul would continually tap the tambourine on his thigh so that Stevie, who freely and fearlessly roamed the stage, exciting his fans with favorites such as "Uptight (Everything's Alright)," "Nothing's Too Good for My Baby" and "I Was Made to Love Her," would know exactly where he was.

If he got too close to the edge of the stage, Paul would tap his tambourine louder so that Stevie would know to stop, change direction or back up.

Through his many appearances at the Uptown, we could see Stevie's development as a songwriter, with several of his musical gems being written in tandem with Paul. I can clearly remember the warm, soulful feeling that enveloped the audience as we all swayed and sang background to their wistful ballad "Hey Love," which to this day remains my favorite Stevie Wonder song.

> *Hey love! May I have a word with you?*
> *I'd like to tell you, just what I've been going through*
> *My nights are so long*
> *As I watch each hour go by,*
> *Hoping and praying that someday I'll be your guy.*

I was in the house when Stevie Wonder, who had long since dropped the word "Little" from his name, celebrated his 18th birthday at the Uptown, singing joyously, playing nearly every instrument on the legendary stage, and telling his frenzied fans that he was craving "some good ole barbecue." "I got some!" shrieked an excited young lady seated a few rows in front of us.

Part of the magic of live theater however, is that things don't always go exactly as planned, and Sam Reed recalled one such occasion saying, "One time Stevie Wonder was there. He was playing his harmonica and he was jumpin' and jumpin', and his conductor Clarence was conducting the band. By the time he turned around, Stevie had wandered over to the side of the stage, and he almost jumped out into the audience! Clarence caught him in mid-air!"

Occasionally, white artists would release records with a distinct R&B edge, captivating black listeners with songs like "Groovin'" by the Young Rascals, "Crystal Blue Persuasion" by Tommy James & the Shondells, "You've Lost that Lovin' Feeling" by the Righteous Brothers and the Soul Survivors' "Expressway to Your Heart," written and produced by Gamble & Huff. While the chitlin' circuit was primarily a showcase for black artists, a white act with a particularly funky flavor could cross over to black radio and earn its way onto the Uptown stage. Although they were basically assured of a rousing reception based on the strength of their hit record, white artists had to "bring it," just like every other act on the circuit. Such was the case for the Magnificent Men, a talented band from the York/Harrisburg region of Pennsylvania, where historically, rhythm and blues has enjoyed a large and loyal fan base.

"In Lancaster County, York County and Dauphin County, which Harrisburg is in—in that Tri-County area, it's always been a heavily concentrated area of interest in rhythm & blues music," said Bob Angelucci, who formed the Magnificent Men, commonly known as the Mag Men, in 1964. "Most of the time, what we were listening to in our youth was rhythm and blues. There wasn't a lot of Beach Boy listeners out here. Nothing against them, but it just wasn't the thing in this area. It's always been a heavy R&B area and it still is to this day, and now it's also into contemporary jazz as well."

Angelucci says that radio played a major role in shaping his interest in the sound and culture of R&B. "There were pop and R&B stations in the area, but the pop stations played a lot of rhythm & blues," he recalled. "And then there was a guy named Toby Young that had a weekend show, and he did some of the best R&B. He did a lot of the album cuts that people never heard before, and he was a guy that was really adventurous. He had a gospel show as well, but he had a show called 'T.Y. at Midnight,' and everybody used to listen to Toby Young at that time, especially us. I kind of lucked out because the seven people that I finally ended up with in the Magnificent Men all had a profound interest in rhythm & blues music."

Eventually, Angelucci and his musical comrades had the opportunity to work with many of the artists that they idolized.

"There was a place called the Raven Teen Club in Central Pennsylvania, in Harrisburg, that was very popular," Angelucci explained. "They brought all the classic rhythm and blues groups in—the O'Jays, the Temptations, Gladys Knight & the Pips, Ruby & the Romantics—and we were the house band there, so we backed all these artists up. That's how we kind of got started."

The soulful, self-contained septet of the Caucasian persuasion was first booked to play the Uptown when their exquisite and inspiring anthem "Peace of Mind," written by lead singer David Bupp and singer Adrian "Buddy" King, hit the airwaves in 1966.

All the things a man could suffer from, I've suffered from
Although things that are rougher come,
I got tougher from.
I know it's just a matter of time.
I'm gonna find peace of mind.

"I can't tell you how great of an experience that was!" Angelucci said during our lively conversation in June 2012. Even now, he lights up like a little boy on Christmas morning at the memory of playing the Uptown, and couldn't stop smiling as he recalled his very first encounter with the powerful Georgie Woods.

"The first time we went into the Uptown Theater, I went in first, and I had to talk to Georgie Woods. I said, 'I'm Bob Angelucci, leader of the Magnificent Men.' He said, 'Are you the road manager?' I said, 'No, I'm the leader and the drummer.' He said, 'I have the Magnificent Men, and they have that song out now called 'Peace of Mind,' and I said, 'Yeah, that's our group on Capitol Records.' He said, 'No, no, no! The Mag Men are 'brothers!' I said, 'We're the Magnificent Men,' and I showed him the album. He said, 'There must be some mistake here. I'm gonna have to talk to some people.' So he talked to both Jerry Blavat and he talked to William Morris Agency, who had booked us at the Uptown Theater.

"After he got off the phone and everything . . . I'll say it exactly like he said it to me . . . he said, 'I'm gonna have to honor the contract, but we cater to black audiences. It's always been classic rhythm & blues out of the Philly area. Those are the type of artists that we bring in.' I said, 'Well, that's what we perform.' He said, 'Well, I'm gonna tell ya. Your white asses better be really good! They'll throw stuff at cha!'"

What ultimately transpired can only be described at one of my most memorable moments at the Uptown. "They weren't sure how to introduce us," said Angelucci, who recalled that Smokey Robinson & the Miracles, Wilson Pickett and Joe Tex were also on the bill. "Normally the curtains are open at the Uptown Theater, and they had closed the curtains on us because we were self-contained and we had to get out there, set up, get behind our instruments and everything. When the curtain opened, like a split second before we started playing, we heard a gasp from the audience. I started the intro to "Peace of Mind" and we came in, and people just reacted great!

As someone who was actually sitting in the audience that day, I can testify that after an initial moment of shock and awe, the Mag Men were embraced, and given the same rousing reception as every other group that put on a passionate, polished performance at the Uptown. It immediately became evident that the "funky white boys" truly believed in the music, and were not just trying to emulate it.

"We weren't sure how we were going to be accepted, OK?" Angelucci said. "Let's face it. We're a white group playing in a market that has had some of the greatest classic rhythm and blues entertainers of all time—at the Uptown Theater! We idolized these people, and to even get on the same stage—to have that opportunity . . . We got that opportunity, and we were accepted!"

Angelucci called the "Mag Men's" groundbreaking performance "one of the greatest events" of the group's musical career saying, "We'd covered a lot of ground in the five years that we were together with all the original members, between '65 and '70. What it actually did was, it helped us gain entry into the chitlin' circuit, which was all the black theaters."

Being part of a rare white act on the chitlin' circuit gave Angelucci a unique perspective, and he recalled, "People were saying, 'You're going to go into some rough neighborhoods, and you're going to be exposed to some things that you haven't been exposed to,' and we never looked at it like that at all. The artists and the performers and everybody, they didn't [either]. As a matter of fact, they were very protective of us."

Angelucci remains as dedicated to the music today as he was as a wide-eyed kid in the '60s. Still an active musician, he heads his own band, Class Act, which counts original Mag Men Jim Seville (bass guitar) and Tom Pane (sax, vocals) among its members, as well as Angelucci's wife, Rita, on lead vocals.

For the local groups that populated Philly's street corners and tiny recording studios, appearing at the Uptown was a goal in itself. Upon making the charts, hometown acts such as the Ambassadors ("I Really Love You"), the Intrigues ("In a Moment") and the Futures ("Breaking Up"), scored a coveted spot in the lineup and the immediate celebrity status that went along with it.

"Whoever had a record that was similar to a hit, because it was a lot of times when people only had one hit, and they would come to the Uptown one time," said Reed. "But if your record continued to be a hit, or you got another hit, then you'd come back again. The more hits you got, the more times you could be at the Uptown."

Sarah Dash, a passionate historian who has kept journals chronicling her eventful career, including her days on the chitlin' circuit with Patti LaBelle & the Bluebelles, recalled her first engagement at the Uptown, which came after the group's successful single "I Sold My Heart to the Junkman" and an exhilarating performance at the Apollo.

"Georgie Woods was the person that put the show together—he and Irv Nahan," said Dash. "I remember distinctly because it was like a run—we did the Apollo and Johnny Nash was on the show. A special night was going to take place because Sammy Davis, Jr. had never played the Uptown Theater, and he was at the Latin Casino. So he came with Altovise—they were not married yet. She was just a dancer.

"I remember the dresses we wore. They were green with white collars and little gold buttons. We didn't have a lot of money, but we had a lot of style," Dash continued, recalling that many of their outfits were purchased at J.C. Penney. "We had people make them, we went to specialized shops and got our little bell bottom pants. We always wore expensive shoes. We would find the most unique, classiest things, and we did the most unique looks of the girl groups. But if you look at the bottom of our dresses, they were all—no matter what height we were—the same length."

For 15 year old Sarah, even being in the presence of the great Sammy Davis Jr. could not trump the excitement of appearing on stage with Georgie Woods, and she recalled, "I would listen to the radio station, WDAS, and know that I'm going to be on a show that Georgie Woods is going to MC! To me, he was the star! I didn't think about us. My vision as a performer? I thought of Georgie Woods. Wow! He's going to let us sing at the Uptown! That was my vision."

While scoring that elusive hit and playing the Uptown was a dream come true for most artists, for some it was like walking into a nightmare. The gig could be particularly hard on local talent, who were subjected to the unforgiving scrutiny of "friends," neighbors and classmates.

North Philadelphia native Barbara Mason wrote the poignant ballad "Yes, I'm Ready" when she was 18 years old. Released in 1965, the song featured Kenny Gamble on backing vocals and is one of the first recordings featuring Earl Young on drums. The hit record led to Mason's first appearance on the Uptown stage. "I had entitled the song 'Are You Ready?'" she recalled. At that time, my manager, Jimmy Bishop, thought it should be in the first person, and he named it 'Yes, I'm Ready.' I was trying to do something about young people my age who didn't really know anything about love, but hopefully they were ready to learn in the right way. I was one of those people. I didn't have much of a teenage years because as soon as the record broke, I was out of my mother's house and gone.

"I was at the Uptown so much!" Mason said. "I was right there, scared as I could be 'cause all the neighborhood kids knew me. When they announced me I was petrified! I think my first appearance was with Inez and Charlie Fox, Gladys Knight & the Pips, Chuck Jackson—those are the three major artists that I remember. I wasn't way down (in the lineup)—I mean 'Yes, I'm Ready' was a big hit, but still, I had a lot to learn, and it was not any formal training from the people that handled me. I mean, I looked OK, and they just sort of put me out there.

"I was there a number of times, but that first time in the mid-sixties, I have to tell you I was petrified because I knew everybody was going to be there—people from the neighborhood, people I went to school with, and I mean they really wore me out. 'Ooh! Look at that wig! That's a wig, ain't it?' I knew they were going to be there. I said, 'I don't know what to do—they haven't told me what to do. I don't know how to come off, take a bow . . .

"And they all got right in front 'cause they all came early! They were right in the front, and they wore me out! First of all, when the record became such a big smash, they went crazy. They were like, 'Barbara? Really?'

"After performing though, and when I came off, I really felt like 'I can do this.' And each show got better because I felt more comfortable. I think having Norman Harris and them behind me really made me feel like, 'I got my homeys with me.' Sam Reed and excellent musicians."

While playing the Uptown was a stepping stone to stardom for the Stylistics, Russell Thompkins, Jr., who has since performed on major stages all over the world while struggling with stage fright, shared Barbara Mason's initial feeling of panic. "I can't say it nicely—I was scared shitless!" he recalled. "I was only about 19 years old then and I didn't have any experience, so I know I was afraid. I was probably so afraid I can't even remember it!

"I've always had a little bit of stage fright. I still get that way, especially when I work at home, but I have more control over it now," Thompkins said. "It's nothing that actually stops me. But when I was young, I used to go on stage and my leg would start jumping and it wouldn't stop! Normally it would take me about two songs to get used to it. Once I got a couple of songs out I'd come around."

A former studio background singer who earned the distinction of becoming "the first Black female teen idol," Dee Dee Sharp, born Dione LaRue, grew up at 27th and Gordon streets in North Philadelphia, and made her Uptown debut based on the success of her number one smash, "Mashed Potato Time," released in 1962. Like Mason and Thompkins, Sharp was one of many talented teens to emerge from the community surrounding the Uptown.

She was the darling of Philly's thriving Cameo label, headquartered at 309 S. Broad St., the historic location of Gamble & Huff's Philadelphia International Records before an arson fire in February 2010 temporarily shut down its offices. A frequent guest on Dick Clark's "American Bandstand," Sharp was being groomed as a pop star and did not tour the chitlin' circuit with her contemporaries. However, she was well aware of the prestige and experience that came with playing venues such as the Uptown and the Apollo.

"I've worked the Uptown so many times that I can't even remember how many times I've worked it!" said Sharp, who was married to Kenny Gamble, producer of several of her singles, from 1967 to 1980. "The first time I worked the Uptown Theater I was 16 years old, almost 17, and I was scared out of my gourd! I was working with the Isley Brothers, Tommy Hunt, Chuck Jackson, and I learned a lot from Jerry Butler. I learned a lot from Chuck Jackson—the technique, and the way they actually connect with the audience. It's a beautiful feeling to know that you're connected with the audience. It's just a wonderful feeling and they showed me how to do that, 'cause I didn't know nothing! I didn't know squat!

"The Uptown audience was rough! If you weren't good, they'd tell you about it. If you made a mistake, they'd tell you about it. It's just like the Apollo. If you can work the Apollo, and I've worked it many times, you can work the Uptown. The people at the Uptown are real folks. They don't pull no punches. They will let you know if they enjoyed you, and if they didn't, they won't say nothing!"

Dee Dee Sharp's close friend Ernest Evans, who rose to pop music prominence as Chubby Checker, recounted the most vivid tale of Uptown terror. Though his name is closely identified with Philadelphia, Checker was actually born in South Carolina and moved to South Philly when he was seven years old. His 1959 cover of the Hank Ballard tune, "The Twist," started a nation-wide dance craze, but it was a minor novelty hit titled "The Class," in which Checker performed various impersonations, that reached No. 36 on the charts in 1959, and resulted in his one and only appearance at the Uptown. The memory of that experience still caused the veteran entertainer to grimace and squirm in his chair when he shared it with me in January 2011.

"I was like a rabbit in a pit of snakes—the best way to describe it!" Checker said. "I played the Uptown and I had this very stupid record—I wasn't having fun. It was called 'The Class.' My first record was a hit and I had to go in front of all of those R&B singers and sing this song. Georgie Woods was the disc jockey and I was the first one to go on, and I was singing 'The Class.' Part of the song was 'Mary Had a Little Lamb,' and I was singing that at the Uptown. It was very painful."

Adding insult to injury, Checker was required to lead off a top-notch lineup of R&B all-stars. "That's why I felt so bad," he said. "Listen to this—Isley Brothers, Flamingos, Jerry Butler, Jesse Belvin, Ray Peterson and Chubby Checker. I'll never forget it! Jerry Butler was singing 'For Your Precious Love' and Curtis Mayfield was playing guitar for him, and I was singing 'The Class.' The Flamingos were singing, *Shoo-wop, shoo-wop!* ("I Only Have Eyes for You"). And the Isley Brothers . . . *you make me wanna shout!* And I'm singing 'Mary had a little lamb!' That wasn't fun!"

While his onstage experience left a bad taste in his mouth, Checker's feelings of inadequacy continued even after the curtain closed. "I was trying to befriend Georgie Woods—he didn't even want to know about me. That made me feel worse!" he said. "It's just that I liked Georgie Woods, and when I went to see him, he just didn't pay too much attention to me at all. I first met him at the Uptown, but the whole time Georgie was around, he never really . . . it's alright. He never played my record of 'The Twist.' He always played Hank Ballard's." Fortunately 18 months later, in June of 1960, "The Twist" became a No. 1 hit, making the whole Uptown ordeal a bit more palatable—somewhat.

A particularly provocative production offered to Uptown patrons was the glitzy Jewel Box Revue, a famous touring company of female impersonators that began in 1939 and ran until 1973. Longtime lovers Danny Brown and Doc Benner owned, operated and produced the spectacular revue, which counted Sammy Davis, Jr. among its fans.

Featuring jaw-dropping impersonations of stars such as Pearl Bailey, Tallulah Bankhead, Katherine Hepburn, Bette Davis and Claudette Colbert, the Jewel Box Revue was billed as "25 Men and a Girl," with the lone female being the famous male impersonator Storme De Laviere. To this day, Reed has vivid memories of the lavish and wildly entertaining drag show.

"One time I was there and they had the Jewel Box Revue. The whole show was built around them, and everybody in there was male, but you'd have like Billie Holiday," he recalled. "We didn't play on stage that time. We were out in front, so they asked me would I participate in the show. I didn't know what I was gonna say, but I said, 'Okay,' 'cause I was the bandleader. So when the thing went down, we'd play a couple of notes and they'd start singing then go, 'Stop! Stop! Stop!' He'd say, 'What do you have there?' and I was supposed to say, 'I don't have a thing. I don't have *a thing!*' And he said, 'Oh! You *don't?!*'"

Music lovers gather at The Uptown for one of Georgie Woods' great R&B shows. Photo: Weldon McDougal, III

The Uptown Theater was a place to see and be seen. L-R: NBA great Julius "Dr. J" Erving, Sam Reed and Henry Evans, the longtime road manager for Teddy Pendergrass. (Courtesy of Sam Reed)

L to R: Jerry Bolding (DJ at WWRL NYC), Stevie Wonder, Weldon McDougal III. (Courtesy of Weldon McDougal, IV)

Sonny Hopson (left) of WHAT and Ray Charles, backstage at the Uptown. Photo: Weldon McDougal, III (Courtesy of Weldon McDougal, IV)

Little Willie John, best known for the hit "Fever," was among the many dynamic entertainers that played the Uptown Theater. (Courtesy of Sepia Magazine/Kevin John)

Young Mavis Staples in the recording studio. (Photo: "Rejoice & Shout," a Magnolia Pictures release. From the Michael Ochs Archive c Getty Images.)

Uptown icons: Legendary Philadelphia drummer Earl Young (left), founder of the Trammps, and beloved balladeer Jerry "The Iceman" Butler. (Courtesy of Earl Young)

Music moguls Kenny Gamble (seated, center), Jimmy Bishop (standing) and Leon Huff (seated, right) enjoy a light moment with the O'Jays. Photo: Weldon McDougal, III. (Courtesy of Weldon McDougal, IV)

Comedian Dap Sugar Willie "from North Philly" made it to the Uptown stage before winning a recurring role as "Lenny" in the popular 70s sitcom, "Good Times." Photo: Weldon McDougal, III (Courtesy of Weldon McDougal, IV)

The exotic and soulful Linda Jones, best known for the R&B classic, "Hypnotized." (Courtesy of Terry Jones)

The Temptations in WHAT studio with disc jockey Sonny Hopson.
Photo: Weldon McDougal, III (Courtesy of Weldon McDougal, IV)

The Trammps (formerly The Volcanoes), Martha & the Vandellas and Weldon McDougal backstage at the Uptown. (Courtesy of Weldon McDougal, IV)

The Magnificent Men, who hail from the Harrisburg/York region of Pennsylvania, made their auspicious Uptown debut on the strength of their smooth soul classic, "Peace of Mind." (Courtesy of Robert Angelucci)

Before his career took off with his version of Hank Ballard's "The Twist," Chubby Checker appeared at the Uptown on the strength of his hit single, "The Class". (Courtesy of Chubby Checker/Mary Parisi)

Philadelphia native Dee Dee Sharp, who became known as "the first Black female teen idol," made her Uptown debut based on the success of her #1 smash, "Mashed Potato Time." (Courtesy of Louis Bolling)

Rock and Roll Hall of Fame inductee Jerome "Little Anthony" Gourdine of Little Anthony & the Imperials has fond memories of playing at the Uptown Theater. (Courtesy of George Dassinger.)

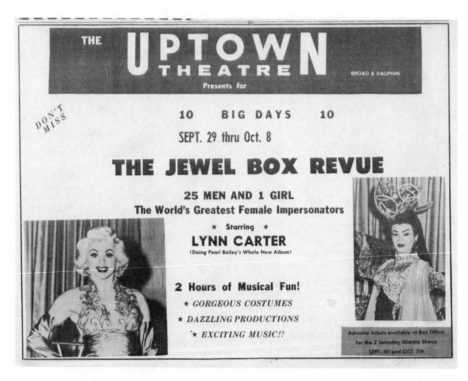

A newspaper ad announcing The Jewel Box Revue at the Uptown. (Courtesy of JD Doyle, QueerMusicHeritage.com)

ROBBIN ROGERS

Female impersonator Robbin Rogers, one of the stars of The Jewel Box Revue, a popular attraction at the Uptown. (Courtesy of JD Doyle, QueerMusicHeritage.com)

MINNIE OF THE GOLDEN WEST

The Jewel Box Revue, a campy and charismatic troupe of female impersonators, presents a spectacular production of "Minnie of the Golden West." (Courtesy of JD Doyle, QueerMusicHeritage.com)

At the Uptown's testosterone-fueled "Battle of the Groups," the Delfonics struck fear in the hearts of the other worthy contestants. L-R: Randy Cain, William "Poogie" Hart and Wilbert Hart. (Courtesy of William Hart)

The Manhattans were always strong contenders in the Uptown's legendary "Battle of the Groups." Standing: Richard Taylor (left) and Edward "Sonny" Bivins Seated L-R: Winfred "Blue" Lovett, Gerald Alston and Kenneth Kelly. (Courtesy of Gerald Alston)

Patti LaBelle & the Bluebelles during the Uptown's glory days. During the 70's, Nona Hendryx (left), Sarah Dash and Patti LaBelle would transform themselves into the supergroup, Labelle. (Courtesy of Nona Hendryx)

With their first big hit, "United," The Intruders ushered in the new Gamble & Huff sound. L-R: Phil Terry, Eugene "Bird" Daughtry, Sam "Little Sonny" Brown and Robert "Big Sonny" Edwards. (Courtesy of Phillip Terry)

With romantic hits such as "You are Everything" and "Betcha By Golly Wow," The Stylistics were the perfect vehicle for the sophisticated soul of Thom Bell and Linda Creed. L-R: Airrion Love, James Smith, James Dunn, Herb Murrell and Russell Thompkins, Jr. (Courtesy of Russell Thompkins, Jr.)

The Temptations at the Uptown. Photo: Weldon McDougal, III. (Courtesy of Weldon McDougal, IV)

Otis Williams (left) and Melvin Franklin (right) of The Temptations on the Uptown stage. Photo: Weldon McDougal, III. (Courtesy of Weldon McDougal, IV)

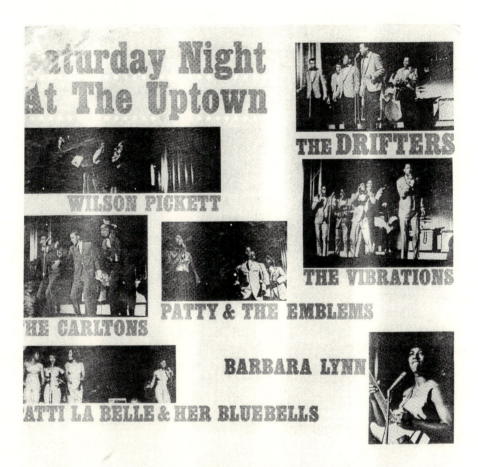

The 1964 Atlantic Records release "Saturday Night At The Uptown," one of the rare concerts recorded live at the historic Philadelphia landmark.

7

Battle Of The Groups

Grease Paint and Girls Gone Wild!

THE MOST STRATEGIC and effective promotional tool employed by Georgie Woods was the "Battle of the Groups," pitting several handsome, talented and fiercely competitive male vocal groups against each other in an all-out testosterone-fueled war. Judged by the audience on everything from costumes to choreography, the victor had supreme bragging rights until the next monumental Uptown showdown.

The deciding factors were usually: 1) which lead singer had the sweetest falsetto 2) which lead singer was the best at dropping to his knees and begging and 3) which group had the best choreography and the sharpest "flams."

Flams were quick, staccato movements done in sync with coordinating rim shots on the snare drum. They were usually placed at the most emotional part of a song, and designed to get the maximum amount of passionate screams from the females in the audience. Even the guys in the house gave props to groups with tight flams, then went home to practice them. The Temptations, of course, were the masters.

"Most of the singers sang for the ladies," said Earl Young. "It was competition! It was about who had the prettiest clothes, hair and makeup. I mean, the guys had more makeup than what women wear! Packed! Those guys came out pretty! You couldn't see no shaving marks! It was a thing called grease paint, and I remember they used to sell it, 'cause the guy asked me to go get it. It was on 10th & Chestnut. It was a stage place, and he needed some grease paint. I said, 'Grease paint?' And they packed that on there, boy . . . If they walked out onstage and the girls didn't scream, you're dead! Don't sing, just walk out. If they don't scream when you walk out there, you're done!"

Whether it was the Manhattans lamenting "I'm the One Love Forgot," the Mad Lads commanding "Come Closer to Me," or the O'Jays swearing "I'll Be Sweeter Tomorrow," every performance was delivered with precision, passion and power.

"You had to worry about the Manhattans, a really great group, the great Delfonics, the Miracles . . . you had to worry about these people!" Eddie Levert recalled. "The edge that we had was just the soulfulness, because all the rest of those guys, they sang sweet songs, like Ray, Goodman & Brown—the Moments, they had 'Love on a Two-Way Street.' We did 'Look Over Your Shoulder,' 'I'll Be Sweeter Tomorrow'—really gut-wrenching songs that would get down to the nasty part. And remember now, all of those groups were stars within their own right, and you had to earn your way in Philadelphia, 'cause those folks come to that show and they stayed all day long, and they'd talk about you real bad! You could hear 'em sayin' things . . . 'Get off the stage!' and 'Look at those shoes!' They'd talk about your shoes!"

"I loved the competition that we had with the O'Jays," said the Manhattans' Blue Lovett. "The Stylistcs were a little ahead of them—the Delfonics were it! Especially in Philadelphia back then. Ray, Goodman & Brown—they were the Moments back then—they were great friends of ours, and we loved the things that they did.

"But everybody would come back in the dressing room to improve whatever mistakes we made. We weren't satisfied with just the standing ovations, or the people hollerin' and screamin' and stuff. We were business-like with everything that we did. We wanted to improve—get better."

Occasionally, opponents in the battle would present a bit of a distraction while another group was frolicking in front of the footlights, and with great amusement Lovett recalled, "looking down in the [orchestra] pit and seeing two of the lead singers—I'm not going to say who they are—turning up their wine bottles, having a little taste . . . while the show was going on, mind you! It was funny, and we could hardly sing for laughing, and they were messin' with us down there in the pit makin' faces and holdin' the bottles up!"

A pivotal opponent in the battles was the Intruders. Comprised of the incredibly cute Sam "Little Sonny" Brown, Phil Terry, Robert "Big Sonny" Edwards and Eugene "Bird" Daughtry, the Intruders officially ushered in the signature Gamble & Huff sound with their 1966 release, "United."

"I loved the Intruders! That was my favorite group!" said Kenny Gamble. First of all, the lead singer, Little Sonny . . . such a great voice! Such a unique voice! The first show I saw them was down at 40th & Girard. It was called the Dell Theater, and it was a disc jockey Rockin' Robin that was here in Philadelphia. And so, he got the Dell Theater and he gave a show, kind of like the Uptown, in West Philly.

"I went down there, and when I saw the Intruders, I said, 'Boy! These guys are great!' I had no idea then that I would be recording them or working with them, but as things go around, Huff was working with a guy named Leroy Lovett. Leroy Lovett had signed the Intruders to a contract. Me and Huff got together and I said, 'Dag! You got the Intruders! Man, come on! Let me help you write some songs for them!' That's how it began—the relationship with the Intruders." Robert "Big Sonny" Edwards stated, "We got [Gamble] started, "We were first. He would not be on the map if it wasn't for us!"

"April of '66, we had our first 'Billboard' hit, which was 'United,' and we hit consecutively for the next 10 years," said Phil Terry, who is a captivating storyteller, and was personally recommended to me by Gamble for this project. "So 'United' was so big in April that by the time June rolls around, it's like number one on the Black stations.

> *I'm tired of runnin' around.*
> *Me and my baby gonna settle down.*
> *I'm gonna make her my June bride.*
> *We gonna walk down the aisle side by side.*
> *I need her and she needs me.*
> *That's the way it's gonna be.*
> *And Baby, you just wait and see,*
> *We gonna be united!*

"It was such an exciting time!" said Terry. "April, it jumps out there, and every time you turn the radio on, all you hear is 'United.' I couldn't believe it . . . like I was in a dream. And so, July 1, Georgie Woods, Jimmy Bishop—I think they were doing it together—but you have this 'Battle of the Groups' show. You have the Temptations headlining—'Ain't Too Proud to Beg' was number one; the Vibrations, because before the Temptations, the Vibrations would do to the Uptown what the Temptations had just took completely over. You had Gladys Knight & the Pips, you had the Intruders, you had the Mad Lads, you had the Capitols . . . you could not get near the Uptown Theater for 10 days, I mean, literally! The line was going from the front of the box office, all the way 'round Susquehanna and back to that Carlisle Street, and it was like that everyday!"

Now that it has been more than 40 years since the groups faced off on the Uptown stage, the singers tend to downplay the fierce competitive nature of the battles, although at the time, they used every available resource to gain an advantage, including the specialized services of Krass Brothers Men's Store, located at 937 South St. Known as "The Store of the Stars," Krass Brothers Men's Store, owned by Ben, Jack and Harry Krass, was equally well known for its quick and campy commercials in which Ben, upon being attacked by a mugger, would declare, "If you didn't buy your suit from Krass Brothers Men's Store, YOU WUZ ROBBED!"

As corny as that was, it got even worse. In another lightening quick TV spot, Ben, who is lying in a casket in a loud purple suit, suddenly sits up and advises, "If you gotta go, go in a Krass Brothers suit!" Despite his embarrassing, yet strangely entertaining advertising tactics, Krass Brothers was the preferred haberdasher of many Uptown artists.

"So the Intruders are going to be there for 10 days, and we're gonna make $1,000.00 for the 10 days!" Terry recalled. "We all had our little day jobs, right? So we said, 'Benny, here. We gonna give you the thousand dollars. We just wanna be sharp!' And you know what? I'll tell you the truth. That was our legacy—our wardrobe. My goodness! We gave Benny that thousand dollars, and I think we must have got about six or seven changes out of that. As a matter of fact, by the second day, the Temptations had to step back, and the next thing I know, they had us in that room back there because we impressed them so much!

"As a matter of fact, we have become very close, because when we did our 'Cowboys to Girls' album, all five original members—Otis Williams, Eddie Kendricks, David Ruffin, Melvin Franklin, Paul Williams—they all did the liner notes with their signatures on the back of that album!"

"The first show that we did was with the Temptations," said Edwards. We were the co-stars, 'cause we always admired them. They were like big brothers to us, and come to find out that we was on the show—my knees was knockin'! But once the music started playing, everything just flowed into place."

"I'll let you know another secret," said Terry. "We were so clean then, that people just expected the Intruders to be impeccable when it comes to clothing, and little as it may be known, Kenny Gamble was our clothing designer. He designed a lot of those clothes. If you look at a lot of our outfits, you can see how unique they were. We had several tailors in this city here (Philadelphia), and we had a nice tailor in New York City, but on that 'Energy of Love' album, we also went out in California and used Diana Ross' designer. I think he put together an outfit that cost us $1,000.00 an outfit, so we spent $4,000.00 for all that. We had rhinestone shirts."

While in the heat of battle, their romantic ballads "United," "Cowboys to Girls" and "Together" had everyone swaying to the music and singing along, I vividly remember the Intruders' dynamic rendition of "Check Yourself," and Terry revealed that the group had a secret weapon in the form of a Broadway legend.

"Honi Coles helped to put that routine together for us," said Terry. "Honi Coles told us, 'Listen! When they start that 'Check Yourself,' be out there in the wings, and when that drum hits, y'all break outta there like gangbusters!' Honi Coles had us up there on Broadway. We was up on Broadway for a whole week with the mirrors and the whole nine yards!"

"I was very proud when I was sitting in the audience watching the Intruders up there on that stage," said Leon Huff. "During that era, that was the epitome of Philadelphia artists performing."

When it came down to vocal prowess, showmanship and pure swagger, no one could touch the Delfonics, comprised of Philly natives William "Poogie" Hart and his brother Wilbert Hart, as well as Randy Cain, who provided a bit of eye candy during a time when light-skinned brothers were very much in vogue. "They didn't want no parts of us! We had the ladies on lockdown, too!" said charismatic lead singer William Hart, who provided the lyrics for unforgettable ballads such as "La La Means I Love You," "Somebody Loves You," "Didn't I Blow Your Mind This Time" and "Break Your Promise."

Hart's romantic lyrics and distinctive falsetto, combined with Thom Bell's fully-orchestrated melodies and ingenious use of such exotic instruments as the harpsichord and the sitar, gave the Delfonics a unique new sound, and their first collaboration, a bold yet haunting single titled "He Don't Really Love You" was released in 1967.

Hart was 18 years old when "He Don't Really Love You" hit the airwaves, and vividly recalled the experience saying, "When I first heard that record, I was riding down 52nd Street going toward Spruce Street—it was on the air! I think Sonny Hopson was playing it or Jimmy Bishop. And then I would turn from one station and it would be on another station, and I'm thinking to myself, 'Wow! I gotta be dreamin'! This is really happening!' It's a dream that you don't want to wake up from!"

The Delfonics made numerous appearances on the legendary Uptown stage, taking on all comers in Woods' highly publicized vocal challenges.

"The Uptown was home—with your crew, you know? West Philly, North Philly—everybody came," said Hart, who was influenced by Frankie Lymon and Little Anthony. "In the minds of the people it was a battle, so Georgie Woods just called it 'The Battle of the Groups,' "I had not a single soul on the planet that I was worried about! Even when I met Anthony—we did a show with Little Anthony—worried for what? Because I did what I did well, and he did what he did well. I wasn't worried about Stevie Wonder or none of them. Nobody!"

From his unique vantage point at center stage, Earl Young observed that such confidence and charisma had its benefits.

"When you're onstage and you'd be singing, you would throw your key to the person you wanted to be in your room," he explained. "You'd give your hotel key to the girl and she'd meet you there. Everybody carried their keys, and if I checked you out and you were cool, the guy would give you the key and you'd be laying up there when I get there!"

In one of our many interviews that have taken place over the years, Hart, still confident and conscious of his significant contribution to Philly's musical legacy, remembers the Uptown as a place where he would literally be transformed as he waited to step onstage.

"That part is like a real dream," he said in a low, husky voice that is in stark contrast to his signature falsetto. "You know, a dream that you have? The [stage] lights, and it's dark back there, then it's very colored. There's a group out on the stage singing and there's people out there screaming. It was like somebody's dream, because when I go out on the stage, I literally am not the person that you're talking to now. I turn into a totally other person, and most entertainers do. They turn into that person—that entertainer God made them.

"And I'm telling you, of all the songs that I've ever written, if you ask me, 'What's the words to 'Somebody Loves You?' right now, I couldn't run 'em off to you. I would have to hear the band strike up, and I wouldn't forget a word. It's like I'm programmed."

In 1968, the Delfonics released the exquisite ballad "La La Means I Love You," giving the group its first bona fide hit. "Aw Man! I tell you, they couldn't wait, and when we went into it, we had steps prepared for it, and we were ready for 'La La,'" Hart said. "And the girls were just screamin' 'cause we were three tall, handsome guys!"

The same could be said of the Moments of Hackensack, New Jersey, who captivated the ladies with such heavenly hits as "Not On the Outside," "Sunday" and "Somebody Loves You Baby." With a lineup that featured the sweet falsetto of Billy Brown, bass/baritone Al Goodman and Johnny Moore, who was replaced by tenor Harry Ray in 1970, the Moments are best known for their poignant classic "Love on a Two-Way Street," which topped the Billboard R&B chart and climbed to #3 in the pop category.

As two tantalizing trios that delivered seductive love songs, the comparisons between the Delfonics and the Moments were inevitable, setting up a delicious rivalry between the groups.

"Aw yeah! We used to have a thing about who'd come out on the stage the cleanest, and we would always be the sharpest, cleanest group," Hart said. "I remember when Al Goodman used to tell me, 'Poogie, when I first saw y'all, I saw these three guys, and we wanted to be just like y'all.' The Stylistics, they would say the same thing. It was never a battle. We had so much love for one another, and went up and down the road together."

The jovial and outspoken Al Goodman, whom I spoke to at length in 2007, remembered it quite differently saying, "The Moments and the Delfonics had the biggest battles you ever seen in your life at the Uptown Theater!"

After a bit of prodding, Hart did eventually recall the good natured rivalry between the two groups and how much fun it was to keep it going.

"People like controversy," he said. "So we used to get on the radio and I'd say, 'OK. I want you to say something bad about us, and we gonna say something bad about y'all.' So I'd say, 'I'm gonna teach them Moments a lesson!' and Al would say, 'We gonna show the Delfonics that they aint' the only ones that can sing them love songs!'"

"If you remember, there was three and four shows a day," said Goodman. "There were lines around the corner. I think it was Friday,

Saturday and Sunday the Moments and the Delfonics was battling! They had signs . . . 'I love the Moments!' 'I love the Delfonics!'

"Back in that day, I talked to Poogie. I said, 'Poogie, look at that man!' We had had it in New York at the Manhattan Center, and then we took it to the Uptown in Philly. I said, 'Poogie, look at that right there. Man, we could take this all over the country, and while everybody's talking about who won, we'd be up in the room countin' money!' Poogie had such a big ego back in that day—he's mellowed a lot. He told me, 'Listen. Yeah, we can do all of that man, but we'll take 80 percent and you take 20 percent!' And now, 30 years later, when he's cold as a refrigerator and so are we, he said, 'Man, we should do that thing that we talked about years ago!' I said, 'Poogie, you're crazy man! We were hot as pepper back then! It's too late, Poogie. We blew our chance when we had it, with your crazy 80 percent!"

Sadly, Al Goodman, the beloved baritone, passed away in July 2010 at age 67.

With a pure, soaring tenor that proved to be the perfect vehicle for the lush romantic ballads of Thom Bell and Linda Creed, Russell Thompkins Jr. helped put the Stylistics on the charts with crossover hits such as "You Are Everything," "Betcha By Golly Wow" and "You Make Me Feel Brand New." However, it was the success of their first hit, "You're a Big Girl Now," released in 1970, that landed them on the Uptown stage.

"I'll never forget it. I was born around the corner from there on Carlisle and Diamond," said Thompkins. "I used to go see the shows all the time. We used to go on Fridays when they used to have the 50-cent show, and I never had any idea in my mind that I would ever be on that stage."

While most of the combatants in the Uptown's highly-anticipated battles were more than willing to draw first blood, young Thompkins, nearly paralyzed with fear, had a very different approach as he faced off against warriors such as the Futures, and the Ethics. "Back then, you didn't prepare for a battle," the self-effacing singer said during the summer of 2011. "You just tried to put your best foot forward, and hopefully that would be enough, because we really didn't know enough to put something together to fight somebody back. You just put your best foot forward and hoped that the crowd enjoyed it. Even groups that I've always thought were more superior than our group talent-wise or things like that, I never worried about it. I just would go onstage and deliver my message and be comfortable with that."

Thompkins was definitely the exception to the rule at the testosterone-fueled singing smackdowns in which the swagger and hometown supremacy of the Delfonics was most likely to prevail. However, there was one group that absolutely commanded respect, even from the "Supersonic" Delfonics—the Temptations.

Tall, tan, tempting and talented, Eddie Kendricks, Paul Williams, Melvin Franklin, Otis Williams and David Ruffin (who was replaced by Dennis Edwards in 1968) were the undisputed Chocolate Gods of R&B. With an arsenal of hits that included "The Way You Do the Things You Do," "My Girl," "Don't Look Back," "Get Ready" and "Ain't Too Proud to Beg," their steps were tighter, their outfits sharper and their harmonies sweeter than all who dared to challenge them. To compound the situation, each of the soulful stallions was capable of singing lead.

Whether it was the unabashed sexuality of bad boy David Ruffin or the romantic longing of Eddie Kendricks, the Temptations, who were inducted into the Rock and Roll Hall of Fame in 1989, were clearly in a class by themselves, taking the audience on an emotional journey that included the sweet sincerity of the Smokey Robinson composition "My Girl" and the raw soul of Norman Whitfield's "Ain't Too Proud to Beg" . . .

> *I know you want to leave me,*
> *But I refuse to let you go.*
> *If I have to beg and plead for your sympathy,*
> *I don't mind, 'cause you mean that much to me.*

"At the Uptown, we had the Battle of the Groups, when it was the Impressions, the Four Tops, the Vibrations, the Temptations—it was heavyweight shows, and they had all that weight on us, 'cause we had to close," said Otis Williams. "We were being baptized in fire, and that was the original Temps, but we could deal with it. We were good!"

As if the Temps needed any help in distinguishing themselves, they were the innovators of the "four-headed" microphone, which would ultimately become their trademark.

"We were rehearsing, getting groomed to go to the Copacabana, and during one of our rehearsals at Motown Artist Development, we were just sitting around kicking out ideas, and we said, 'We want to be different from any other group,'" Williams recalled. "We want to have something that will make a statement.' David said, 'Yeah man! It would be great if we could get a four-headed mic on one stand!' Lon Fontaine, who was our choreographer said, 'I know some people who can do that.' We said, 'Really?' and he knew somebody that was connected with the 'Star Trek' people. Lon got in touch with them and they made it up, and that was the 'T' in Temptation.

"When they'd put that microphone out there, the place would go crazy! The four-headed mic would be standing in front of the curtain. When they opened the curtain up and saw the five of us standing there—pandemonium!"

One group that proved to be particularly problematic for most acts on the bill was the Vibrations. While their minor hits "Misty," "Oh Cindy," "My Girl Sloopy" and "Love in Them There Hills" never topped the charts, their daring, high-energy stage show made them perennial favorites at the Uptown. Eddie Levert recalled, "They performed so great! They were just a great, great group!" and Sam Reed added, "The Vibrations, they were very popular. They were an acrobatic group. They would sing, then they would do some acrobatics. Just about every show they would be there because they were very popular at the Uptown."

Although their performances weren't billed as "battles," the female singers brought the same competitive spirit to the stage.

"I liked all the girl acts the most—Martha & the Vandellas, the Marvelettes, the Chantals—all of 'em," said Leon Mitchell. "And I'll turn you on to another secret. When you're onstage and these girls are out in front of you, you've got this big, bright spotlight up in the back shining on 'em, and you could see right through their clothes!" "It's all comin' out now!" Earl Young said gleefully.

While the onstage battles between the male groups were nothing short of epic, the rivalry among the females was a bit more subtle, but no less intense. For the ladies, it usually came down to who had the cutest, most lady-like steps, the biggest hair (wigs) and the sexiest costumes, because all of them could sing.

"I think (the competition) was just as strong [as the men]," said Nona Hendryx, the edgy and imaginative Trenton, New Jersey native who wrote the Labelle classics "Get You Somebody New," "Come Into My Life," "Chameleon" and "(Can I Speak to You Before You Go To) Hollywood," as well as the raucous "Messin' with My Mind."

"It had a lot to do with what you were wearing, what your hairstyle was, your song choices . . . especially in the time of doing big ballads like 'You'll Never Walk Alone' or 'Somewhere Over the Rainbow' or 'Oh,

Danny Boy,'" said Hendryx. "The other girl groups, they would find their big ballads, or the big number that they would do. So it was always some competition, and you had to make sure your big ballad wasn't the big ballad that they were doing. Whatever yours was, you owned that. And the thing of where you go on in the lineup—whether you were headlining. Those were the ways we competed with each other.

"I think we had, in the beginning, a real competition with the Shirelles. Patti LaBelle & the Bluebelles, we didn't have the hits that the Shirelles had, so there was a lot of competition in that way." According to Patti LaBelle, one rivalry became particularly heated.

"It was always with the Supremes, you know? We had our moments," she said. "Whatever we wore, if Diana Ross saw it, she would go out and get it. They would go on before us, and to the audience, it would look like we copied the Supremes. It was a lot of rivalry. I guess it was healthy because I grew up into a person that was never competing. I guess that was our graduation. We were enjoying it because everybody else was doing it, and we thought that was the thing to do. If they're going to try and compete, then let's compete!"

In addition to choreographing the Intruders' polished presentation, tap legend Honi Coles also worked his magic with the ladies, providing cute, coquettish routines for Patti, Nona and Sarah. But once again, according to Dash, those sneaky Supremes committed a blatant foul.

"I don't know how we wound up in that Motown show, but there were the Marvalettes, there were Martha & the Vandellas, there were the Supremes and there were Patti LaBelle & the Bluebelles," said Dash. "Patti LaBelle & the Bluebelles were known for doing not only our unique singing, but we also did little time steps and we took classical steps of tap dance and incorporated them in our movements. And we were taught by the best, which was Honi Coles. Honi Coles taught us how to do the time step and a little 'ball change' in our music, and when we would break into it, the audience would just fall on the floor, because we were in high heels and we were doing the ball change and the time step! So it was the first time that some of the Motown females had seen it.

"Well, at that time, Diana and her girls weren't as strong as we were—our notoriety with the city—so they went on first and we were sort of towards the end. Diana and the girls did our steps, and people who had been to see us, they knew that this was part of Patti LaBelle & the Bluebelles. Whenever you saw our show, we included this little bit in our movements, and there they did it, and it didn't go over that well.

They actually had egg on their faces. I don't know whether it was Jimmy Bishop or Georgie Woods, but someone on the side, they were the MC, and [the Supremes] were reprimanded for doing such a thing!"

While they were consummate professionals on stage, all of that testosterone and estrogen emanating from the young, fine and frisky artists on the chitlin' circuit made for plenty of backstage romance and high school-style hijinks. According to Eddie Levert, the time between shows was spent "shooting dice, running around backstage or outside trying to get a girlfriend," and though not one to kiss and tell, even after all these years, Hendryx mused about teenage love affairs that blossomed during a 10-day run at the Uptown, which would last just about that long. "Everybody was in love with Tommy Hunt, Chuck Jackson and Marvin Gaye. I mean, come on! Just teenage crush kind of things." Blue Lovett was equally tight-lipped, only saying, "I had crushes on two people there, but I won't say who!"

With time to kill between shows, or sometimes even during the show, there were plenty of opportunities to make mischief, and the Bluebelles were no exception. "My fondest memory is one of the many times we were there with Curtis Mayfield and the Impressions," said Hendryx. "We had done so many shows with the Impressions for so long that we were like brothers and sisters, and we were pranksters. We would play jokes on each other. You'd be in the theater every day, doing shows all day, and we would do things.

"They went on stage once," she continued, obviously still amused. "And we filled balloons with water and put them in their jackets and in their shoes. And we put newspapers—we just really messed up their stuff! So when they came in to get dressed—'cause a lot of us would come back at the last minute, quickly change, and go on stage. So we messed up them getting on stage, they ran late, Georgie Woods is really upset . . . We laughed and laughed, thought it was funny, and thought that was it.

"And then, at the end of the week—they waited, they were sooo clever and sneaky. They waited 'til then end of the week, and we thought they'd forgotten about what we'd done. And they came in, 'cause Cindy [Birdsong] was with us then, and they stood behind each one of us. It was Curtis and the three guys—Fred, Sam and Jerry. They stood behind us and they sang, 'Goodnight, Sweetheart,' like this beautiful harmony. It was so pretty! We're sitting there going, 'Oh! They're so nice!' And at the end they sang, 'Goodnight, Sweetheart, GOODNIGHT!' And they stuck us all in the butt with pins! We screamed! That's my fondest memory!"

Unfortunately there is no known film footage documenting the creative brilliance and controlled chaos that took place inside the Uptown Theater. However, there are two known sound recordings of it.

In 1964, Atlantic Records released "Saturday Night at the Uptown" (Atlantic 8101), recorded live on July 24, 1964 by Phil Iehle and legendary engineer Tom Dowd. Hosted by Georgie Woods and Jimmy Bishop, the show featured the Drifters, Patti & the Emblems, the ever-popular Vibrations, Wilson Pickett, Patti LaBelle & Her Bluebells, the Carltons and Barbara Lynn.

Highly descriptive liner notes by Bob Altshuler take you inside the theater, where Patti & the Emblems of Camden, N.J. sang their hit "Mixed Up, Shook Up, Girl," co-written by a budding songwriter named Leon Huff. The red hot Drifters sang "Under the Boardwalk" and "On Broadway," substituting the words "Broad Street" for "Broadway" in recognition of the Philly's main thoroughfare, while home girls "Patti LaBelle & Her Bluebells" received a rousing reception for "Down the Aisle."

Another LP, "The Magnificent Men Live!" was recorded at the Uptown Theater in May 1967, and Mag Men founder Bob Angelucci shared the details of the project saying, "We were on Capitol Records at the time, and they asked us about possibly doing a live album—would we consider doing one, and we said, 'Yeah!' We weren't adverse to that at all, and they thought since we had such a great reception at the Uptown Theater, [it] would be great to record there.

"So they contacted Georgie Woods to see if we could get his permission to do so, and what they did was, they ran a big—it looked like one of these big moving van trailers, and that was full of all the processing equipment and recording equipment. They pulled it up right behind the Uptown on the curb, and then they ran all the wiring in the back of the Uptown Theater, and then we did I think it was, if my memory serves me, a Saturday afternoon matinee show that we did. There were a lot of kids there, too. But that was our album. It was live at the Uptown Theater."

8

The Insiders

FROM TOP-LEVEL MANAGEMENT to the lowliest "runner," there was a colorful cast of characters who were responsible for the day-to-day operations of the Uptown, or had unusual behind-the-scenes access to the theater and its stars. I call these intriguing individuals the Uptown "Insiders."

As the inside story of the Uptown unfolded, one name that seemed inescapable was that of Irv Nahan. If the Uptown truly was as magical as the Land of Oz, it appears that Nahan was "the man behind the curtain."

Alleged to have been "hooked up with the gangsters," Irv Nahan was a partner in the Philly-based Red Top Records, founded in 1957 and co-owned by Doc Bagby and Marvin "Red Top" Schwartz. Their roster of artists included Donnie Elbert, The Turbans, the Blue Notes and Screamin' Jay Hawkins.

Nahan also managed the careers of the Drifters, as well as Jerry Butler, who according to Philly native Weldon McDougal III, the pioneering record promotions man who shot many of the historic photographs included here, appeared at the Uptown more than any other act.

The Iceman concurred saying, "We were there quite often. There was a Philadelphia connection, so to speak. I almost moved to Philadelphia at one time. Our offices were there for entertainment purposes. Irv Nahan was managing me, and he had an office over on Spruce Street, so I was in and out of Philadelphia big bunches! He was also the manager for Georgie Woods, and that's probably how that connection came, bringing us into the Uptown probably more than anyone else. Anytime you hear Georgie Woods, Jerry Butler and the Drifters, you'll probably see Irv Nahan's name somewhere in the mix."

"He was the agency for the Uptown Theater—for everything!" Reed said of Nahan. "For the Nixon, for the whole area. He was the man. Whoever records George was playing and they were hot, he would go out and get 'em."

"Irv Nahan once told Bill (Cosby) he would never make it [as a comedian] because he was too clean," Jerry Butler recalled. Cosby, who never worked the chitlin' circuit, does not remember the incident, but bristled when I mentioned it to him saying, "You know, I wasn't even worried about what they were saying, because the feeling was mutual. I was not going to go into a theater and play a place where I am between screaming teenagers who will lose concentration while I'm building on one of my stories and start talking! So I was not about to have that!"

While Nahan clearly had the power, someone else definitely got the glory. Though not actually employed by the theater, the Insider who has proved to be as legendary as some as the artists who have played the Uptown was an enterprising neighbor who lived on Carlisle Street, right behind the theater. A bona fide soul food goddess known simply as "Miss Pearl," she was a valued member of the Uptown family.

"She could really cook that soul food!" Odean Pope exclaimed. "She was directly in back of the stage on Carlisle Street, and all the musicians—everybody—used to eat there. We'd do a matinee show, and between that and the early show, we'd go over there and have some lunch and the food was out of sight! She was something very special."

While Dee Dee Sharp never indulged in Miss Pearl's flavorful fare, she was well aware of this savvy businesswoman's importance to the Uptown's daily operations.

"Since we lived in North Philadelphia, I didn't have no problem with getting food because my family would always cook and bring it to me," she said. "But other folks had to rely on Miss Pearl, and Miss Pearl used to [cook] the food, and then at the end of the week she would stand at the stage door and she would say, 'You owe me so-and-so, and *you* owe me so-and-so, and *you* owe me so-and-so,' and they had to pay it."

Even so, Miss Pearl's high profile customers clearly weren't complaining, and to the dynamic and demonstrative Eddie Levert, dining at her table was about much more than grabbing a bite between shows. It was an experience that bordered on the surreal.

"We used to spend almost all our money eatin' her food!" he recalled. "You could go in there, and there would be Redd Foxx, Dick Gregory,

Smokey Robinson, James Brown—you name it! All of those people would sit at Pearl's table and eat! I mean that, to me, is the richest heritage of my whole life, to be able to say that I was a part of that! Jimmy Bishop, Georgie Woods . . . all those people! I'm just elated to even be around to be able to say something about it, and I really miss those days!"

Little Anthony was also in awe saying, "We used to go across the street to Miss Pearl's. When you'd go to Miss Pearl's, who's in the living room? You'd walk by and there's James Brown sittin' there eatin' some chicken. Oh! There's Jackie Wilson having some greens. Can you imagine these people? How do you repeat that?"

"I really enjoyed the Uptown, because you'd go out backstage and you'd go right across the street to this lady's house. Girl, it was the best!" said Mavis Staples." You couldn't wait for time to go, 'cause that woman could cook! She cooked soul food! Girl, we'd go over there and eat, and then we're ready to do three or four more shows!

From the friends and fellowship to the fashion and food, Staples clearly embraced every moment of her Uptown experience, even when things went awry, and during one of our many conversations, the fond memory of one particularly determined Insider gave her a serious case of the giggles.

"Did I tell you about the little boy, Gary, who ran away from home trying to come where I was?" she asked. "From Philadelphia! His mother finally found me. She said, 'Miss Staples, is Gary with you?' I said, 'No, ma'am!' She said, 'Well, Gary has run away, and he's coming to Chicago!'

"Gary was about 12 years old, but when I first met him, he was eight years old," Staples recalled. "I met Gary at the Uptown Theater backstage, and he and another little girl named Kathy, they were runners for us. They would run to the store for us, so we would get 'em in. They'd come to the back door and we would let 'em go through the theater. They were kids.

"He fell in love! He fell in love with us—with me and the whole family, but mainly me. You know, I took him like a little son, and he wanted to be with me. He just loved me so much! [His mother] said, 'Gary loves you so much, Miss Staples! He's run away from home! He left a note saying he's gone to where Mavis is!' Girl, I got so scared, and finally they found him. Gary had gotten to the train station or somewhere, but he was back at home and I was glad of that."

Fortunately the story has a happy ending, and to this day, Staples has pleasant memories of her pint-sized pal from The City of Brotherly Love.

"He was a little kid and he would come to the Uptown Theater, but I've seen Gary since he's grown," she said in amazement. "Gary's married and he has some children. I have pictures of that little kid when he was a kid, girl!

"I haven't seen Kathy anymore, but maybe about six years ago we were at some outdoor place, and Gary, he said, 'Mavis! It's Gary!' I couldn't believe it, girl! A l'il grown man now! You know what? I can't think of Gary's last name. I just know 'Gary,' and I have a beautiful picture of Gary and my sister and I kissing him on both cheeks. It's beautiful—in my scrapbook!"

While no one knew it at the time, one Insider would become a partner in one of the most prolific songwriting teams in the history of popular music and eventually be inducted into the Rock and Roll Hall of Fame. Before joining forces with Leon Huff, Kenneth "Kenny" Gamble was relentless in his efforts to break into the Uptown in-crowd and ultimately, the music business.

"My first experience with the Uptown, I used to come from South Philly to go up there, and I always used to go by myself so that I could hide when the shows were over," said Gamble, whose deep affection for the theater is still very much in evidence. "If you go with a whole lot of people, you can't get in! So I used to try to stay for all the shows. Eventually, I started going out to WDAS and I got to meet Georgie Woods. I used to go to the store for him and try to wiggle my way into the music scene, and then when I used to come to the Uptown, I used to come backstage. Sometimes they'd let me in, sometimes they wouldn't. It all depends on who was at the door.

"And so I finally got to the point where Jimmy Bishop, who was my real good friend, he'd tell them, 'Let Gamble in when he comes up,' and I was able to get in. I did the same thing at the Uptown. I used to go to the store for him—get chicken sandwiches over at Pearl's, and I got to know Pearl real good.

"Then, the older I got, I started picking people up. I'd use Bishop's car and pick people up. My big story at the Uptown is this. When I first got my car—I had my band [Kenny Gamble & the Romeos]—I had a station wagon. I had just brought this station wagon, so I was at the Uptown and Bishop said, 'Gamble! Smokey Robinson is coming in at the airport. Can you go pick him up?' I said, 'Yeah! I'll pick him up!' I didn't even know where the airport was!

"So I tried to find the airport, right? It seemed like it was so far away! During that time, I don't think they had the expressway or nothing like that, but I'm trying to find the airport, and to this day, me and Smokey, we laugh about it.

"And so, I finally get there and I picked him up—put him in my little raggedy Chevy, and when I started driving he said, 'Can you drive, man?' I said, 'Yeah. I just started drivin'.' He said, 'Now, take it easy, man!' and he was laughin' and I'm so excited to be in the car with Smokey Robinson! I mean, this guy was one of my heroes! Well by the time we got back to the Uptown, he said, 'Thank God, man! We got here safe!' I told him then, I said, 'Man, I want to write songs,' and he said, 'Well, keep trying, man!'"

It appears that Gamble has since had the opportunity to redeem himself, because when I reminded Robinson of the harrowing, yet hilarious incident he responded, "Kenny is my brother! He's picked me up many times!"

Working quietly in the shadows of the theater, mostly seen but not heard, was an Insider whom Leon Mitchell referred to as "The Phantom of the Uptown." Known only as "Moo-Moo," he was often sent to retrieve missing artists and perform a variety of tasks that kept the Uptown machine moving.

"Little Moo-Moo," a nostalgic Odean Pope mused. "He was kind of handicapped, and he was always on the scene. He would run errands for Georgie Woods and Georgie Woods would maybe give him $1.00 or 50 cents. He would maybe go to Pearl's and pick up something for Woods, or go down to the store to pick up something for the musicians. But he would always be there. I had almost forgot about him!"

Not so for Blue Lovett, who clearly was amused by his vivid memories of the Uptown's most industrious Insider.

"There was a little maintenance guy there named Moo Moo," he said. "He was putting up an advertisement for the next show coming in—like those little paper throwaways—and had this huge nail and a hammer! He was in the back by our dressing room hittin' this nail, I mean *nailin' it* into the wall downstairs! We got a big kick out of that, 'cause you could put it in with a thumb tack! He had this big nail, and he was poundin' this advertisement of the next comin' show, or whatever it was! And he was crazy about me. He used to call me 'Boo.' He'd say, 'Boo! Phone call! Boo! Phone call!'"

While the helpful handyman was widely known for his gentle and cheerful persona, Lovett recalled an incident in which Moo Moo's behavior was completely—and perhaps justifiably out of character.

"The same Moo Moo, Wilson [Pickett] did him wrong," he said. "I'm not talking about him 'cause he's not here anymore, but they did something wrong to Moo Moo, and Moo Moo threw some paint on (Pickett's) Rolls Royce out on the street. All of Philadelphia jumped on Wilson for that." Though Moo Moo was implicated in the ugly incident, there is strong speculation that others may have been involved, and Kenny Gamble shared this story . . .

"We recorded Wilson Pickett, right? 'Don't Let the Green Grass Fool You,' so I asked Wilson, 'Have you ever played the Uptown?' and he said, 'I never played it.' I said, 'You've got to play the Uptown.' So I called George and Bishop and I said, 'Hey! Can you put Wilson on at the Uptown?'

"So he played the Uptown—he had a big record and everything. So he had this big, gigantic Rolls Royce, and he parked his Rolls Royce outside the Uptown on that little back street. So he gets in an argument with some of these young brothers out there. He's talkin' about, 'Man, I'm gonna hurt them!' I said, 'You'd better leave these boys alone from up in North Philly! They're not bothering you. They probably admire you!' But he was a real hot head.

"And so he called me up one day . . . 'Gamble! You gotta come up here! What you done got me into?!' I said, 'What happened? I ain't get you into nothin'!' So he said, 'Come on up here, man! They tryin' to hurt me!' So I get up there, and guess what happened? They had taken paint and threw it all over that Rolls Royce! All over that beautiful Rolls Royce! He almost cried!"

The Mag Men's Bob Angelucci's memories of playing the historic venue on Broad Street include its mysterious "Phantom."

"They did refurbish the Uptown Theater one time before," he said. "I think it was in the '80s, because I went down there at that time to meet with people about it. I had the same interest—'If they reopen it, I'd like to [perform there].' There was an elderly gentleman at the time, and he was a lot older by the time I got down there in the early 80s—they used to call him 'Moo-Moo.' He was always there. When I went down there in the early 80s, God bless him, he was still alive and he said, 'Mag Men! Mag Men!' He was a sweetheart. He was just a very kind person."

Perhaps the most captivating inside story was shared by Gilda Woods, even though she wasn't employed by the Uptown, and initially had zero interest in being there at all. However, I got completely caught up when Georgie Woods' elegant widow gave me a charming but very juicy account of how she met the dashing deejay. It appears that even "The Guy with the Goods" was not immune to the magic and the mystique of the majestic theater.

"My girlfriend and I—she lived right on the corner and I lived in South Philly—she said, 'Oh, they've got gorgeous songs and people in there and everything,'" Gilda recalled during our lengthy and engrossing interview in 2005, the year her legendary husband passed away. "I said, 'Oh no! I'm not going in there. I'm kind of scared.' She said, 'No, it's really nice.' I said, 'I'll try it,' and I went to see Tina Turner. There were other people there, but she was the big star then.

"We thought it was so fine and really nice, and when my girlfriend and I were getting ready to leave, this guy, which was not George, said, 'Could you step out a minute?' I said 'Who?' and he said, 'The two of you.' I said, 'Why?' and he said, 'Somebody would like to talk to you.' I said, 'Okay,' and it was George.

"He said, 'Can I take you all out for something to eat?' and my girlfriend said, 'Yeah! Yeah!' and I'm hittin' her and everything. We went out and we had something to eat, and he said, 'Would you like to come here again?' and 'Can I have your number?" And I said to [my girlfriend], 'Don't say anything to him!' I said, 'Yeah,' and I gave him a false number. But he found somebody, and he came over to my house!

"He rang the doorbell, and I thought, 'What the heck is he coming here for?' and I said, 'Mom! Tell him I'm not here!' and she said, 'No, I'm not!' And he just sat there, and he said, 'You know, you don't have to lie!' I said, 'Well, I'm sorry,' and he said, 'Goodbye!' He walked away, and I didn't see him for a while.

"Then the Supremes were going to be there, and I went to see the Supremes," Gilda said, continuing with her intriguing love story. "He saw me out there and he had the guy call me back there along with my girlfriend. It wasn't nice, but he said, 'I'm sorry that I acted that way, but all you had to do was say you didn't want to be bothered.' So I said, 'Did you want me to say it now, or what?' and he said, 'Don't be so smart!' I was liking him, but some girlfriends said, 'He has a lot of women!' I heard all that mess and I think he did have a couple of women.

"But then, he was such a nice guy with my mother and everything. 'Cause my dad died before he knew him that well, and he was as nice to my mother and my family." Gilda married Georgie Woods in October 1963.

James Brown performs on the Uptown stage while Georgie Woods (right) enjoys the show. (Courtesy of Weldon McDougal, IV)

Both as a musician and as a songwriter, trombonist Fred Wesley made a vital contribution to the James Brown sound. (Courtesy of Jonathan Block)

Yours truly with Rock and Roll Hall of Famer Bootsy Collins in his dressing toom on June 25, 2011, after a concert at the Keswick Theatre in Glenside, PA. Collins spent 11 months as a member of James Brown's Band, The J.B's. Photo: Jeff Price

A rare portrait of young Michael Jackson, taken by Philly music pioneer Weldon McDougal before the madness ensued and Jackson was just a normal little boy playing with his yo-yo. Photo: Weldon McDougal, III.

After leaving Motown and brother Jermaine behind in 1976, the Jacksons signed with Gamble & Huff's Philadelphia International Records. Before "I Want You Back," their first Motown release, the group, then known as the Jackson Five, played the Uptown Theater, upstaging headliners such as The Five Stairsteps. L-R: Tito, Joe Jackson, Randy, Michael, Leon Huff, Kenny Gamble, Marlon and Jackie. (Courtesy of Kenny Gamble)

Michael Jackson at the Waldorf Astoria in New York City on March 19, 2001, after being inducted into the Rock and Roll Hall of Fame as a solo artist. Photo: Jeff Price

Here, I'm having a media moment with iconic WDAS air personality, the late Joseph "Butterball" Tamburro, who often hosted the R&B shows at the Uptown Theater. "Butter" took great pride in the fact that he was the first to play Michael Jackson's "Thriller" in the Philadelphia market when no one else had access to the highly anticipated album.

9

The Godfather of Soul & The King of Pop

WHILE EVERY SHOW at the Uptown was a major event in Philadelphia's Black community, nothing could match the excitement and anticipation of the coming of the Godfather of Soul—James Brown.

With an arsenal of hits that included "I Got You," "Please, Please, Please," "Papa's Got a Brand New Bag," "Cold Sweat," "It's a Man's Man's World," "Licking Stick-Licking Stick" and "Get Up (I Feel Like Being a) Sex Machine," Brown's creativity, confidence and pure soul power kept audiences spellbound as he "Camel Walked" his way into our hearts. Trumpeter Wilmer Wise of the Sam Reed Orchestra had a very interesting story to share about the first of Brown's many appearances at the Uptown.

"James Brown, when he came, nobody knew James Brown, but there was a picture of James Brown where his complexion was flawless and he was looking off into space. His hair was perfect," Wise recalled. "So when James hit the stage, his face was pock-marked, the hair was all over the place, and the audience was convinced that they were being ripped off—until he opened his mouth. He looked nothing like his pictures!"

Whether he was delivering a soulful interpretation of the romantic standard "Prisoner of Love" or making a bold statement like "Say It Loud—I'm Black and I'm Proud!" we all marveled at Brown's smooth moves and the command that he had over his incomparable band, which over the years included William "Bootsy" Collins on bass and Fred Wesley on trombone, as well as drummer Melvin Parker and his brother Maceo, a sizzling saxophonist whom Brown frequently called on by name in soul classics such as "Cold Sweat" and "Papa's Got a Brand New Bag!" . . . "Blow Maceo!"

"Man, I'm telling you, anytime you get a chance to be on stage with a James Brown or somebody of that magnitude, it's priceless, although we never knew that we were charting courses and were pioneers or anything like that," Maceo Parker said of his tenure with Brown, who was inducted into the Rock and Roll Hall of Fame in 1986. "But we knew we were working with James Brown and we knew what kind of impact he had on that kind of music, to a point where anytime you knew that James Brown is coming to town, it wouldn't be, 'Are you going?' The question would be what you wear, because it was automatic that you were going!

"So we, the members of the band, got to have that feeling. There's this kind of buzz that James Brown carries with him that's very, very exciting, and the fact that I had my brother (Melvin)—you had two boys out of the same family? You'd just walk around with your chest stuck way out, proud of the fact that you're working with James Brown. All the accolades—'The Hardest Working Man in Show Biz . . .'"

That sentiment was echoed by Bootsy Collins, who joined the band as a phenomenal 18 year-old bass player from Cincinnati, Ohio, following an ugly pay dispute and the subsequent mutiny and departure of several key members. "It was 1970 and I played with him until '71, and the first major hit was 'Sex Machine,'" said Collins, who replaced Bernard Odom and Charles Sherell on bass when he joined the James Brown Band along with his brother, guitarist Phelps "Catfish" Collins. At that time, the name of the unit was changed to the J.B.'s, and with Brown putting his rambunctious young bass player front and center on hits such as "Super Bad," "Give It Up or Turn It Loose," "Soul Power," and "Talking Loud and Saying Nothing," the Collins brothers helped to usher in the funk-fueled sound of the 70s.

"Before we got with James Brown, we played behind a bunch of James Brown wannabes, so we never thought that we'd actually one day be playing behind the real James Brown," the fun-loving Bootsy Collins said in 2011, as he toured the country promoting his CD, "Funk Capital of the World." "It probably took us the whole year for us to realize, 'Dag! I'm actually playing with the real James Brown!' The idea of being in the same room with him was just unreal, and I probably didn't realize 'til after we left how deep that was."

It was with Brown that Collins and his colleagues were introduced to Soul Brother No. 1's trademark concept of playing "on the one," accenting the first beat of the measure, rather than the second and fourth beats. "He was the most innovative musician in the world, and I learned from him," said musician/composer Fred Wesley, who joined the James Brown Band in 1968 and contributed songs like "Pass the Peas" and "The Big Payback" to Brown's repertoire.

As he slid, gyrated and did "the splits," pausing just long enough to command his band to "Hit me!" James Brown and the Uptown Theater proved to be a potent combination, having a profound influence on a young Philly native who would grow up to be one of the most accomplished and recognizable musicians in the country.

"I loved the Uptown Theater! It was after a concert that I saw James Brown in that I wanted to play guitar," said Kevin Eubanks, who spent 18 years as the musical director and bandleader for "The Tonight Show with Jay Leno," before vacating the position on May 28, 2010 to pursue other opportunities. "Oh yeah! The Uptown Theater was very important in my career. I was playing violin up to that point and I saw James Brown at a show there, and when I left the Uptown Theater, I remember standing on the curb saying, 'I want to play guitar!' From that day on I wanted to be a guitar player. You would think that I'd want to be a dancer or singer after seeing James Brown, but I wanted to play guitar."

Eubanks, who comes from a musical family that also includes renowned trombonist Robin Eubanks, brothers Duane and Shane, who play trumpet and trombone respectively, and uncle, piano great Ray Bryant, was inducted into the Philadelphia Music Alliance Walk of Fame in August 2010, taking his place among such luminaries as Gamble & Huff, Thom Bell, John Coltrane and Marian Anderson, and becoming the 113th inductee to be recognized with a bronze pavement marker on Philadelphia's Avenue of the Arts (South Broad Street), between Locust and Spruce Streets.

With unmatched precision and professionalism, the James Brown Band responded to their leader's every hip thrust, head-bob, knee drop and icy stare without missing a beat, or they paid the price—literally. It has been well documented that Brown was notorious for levying fines against band members who dared to deliver anything less than perfection on stage. From improper attire to musical mistakes, every infraction came with a penalty.

"If you ever seen him ball his fist up then fling his [five] fingers out like he was flipping something out of his hand, that's what a fine was," Parker recalled with some amusement. "Like somebody's playing and they go 'Bop!' and somebody goes 'Bop! Bop!' James would look at them, and each one of those would be five dollars. That's your fine. And he had somebody commissioned to stand on the sideline and watch him for the whole show, and if he fined somebody then that person would write it down so he wouldn't forget!"

Even their wardrobe was under tough scrutiny, and Brown was particularly stealthy as he conducted his onstage inspections. "We used to have patent leather shoes and we had to keep 'em greased," Parker explained. "You know when James was bent over and walkin' around like he was crying? He was looking at shoes to see whose grease had came off!"

"We all took pride in doing things correctly," said Fred Wesley, who is probably best known for his free-wheeling trombone solo in "Funky Good Time," co-written by Wesley and Brown. "James would fine sometimes for unnecessary things, but it would usually be for something, and it would be like a joke. The band took pride in playing the parts right and making the hits right—everything done correctly. The band really wanted to do it right. It was a tight band and we took pride in that."

Offstage, Brown was no less intense, and Sam Reed recalled, "He was basically to himself a lot because they had a special room for him, and he mainly just had his crew comin' in and out. As for anybody else there, he wasn't friendly with. In fact, our first little thing—it was basically jokingly though . . . Just when I took over the Uptown, I was just there as the house leader. I was there to see that the shows went alright, and I was supposed to be checking all the union cards as far as the musicians. So they gave him the contract that he was supposed to be paying me my salary [and] he called me in the dressing room and said, 'What do you do here? You don't play no horn or nothin'?' I said, 'I do play the saxophone.' He said, 'Do I really have to give you this money?' I said, 'Yes, you do!' He didn't want to pay 'cause I wasn't part of the show. I was just there as the union representative. He didn't really mean it that way, but he was just talking to me because he had to give me some money, so he wanted to know who he was giving it to.

"But he basically stayed to himself. He would come out every now and then. He'd speak to everybody, but he wasn't one of those that socialized with everybody around him. And Mr. Nash, the stage manager, they might talk a little bit, but other than that, he didn't say much to nobody."

Eventually, the bold and imaginative Bootsy Collins, whose outrageous bass lines could no longer be ignored, found all of the rules and sanctions to be a bit too restrictive, and left the J.B's after only 11 months. Now known simply as "Bootsy," he would soon find a home with George Clinton's Parliament-Funkadelic (P-Funk), where individuality was encouraged and his innate funk factor was more than welcome. Collins formed the zany Bootsy's Rubber Band in 1976, logging funk classics such as "Stretchin' Out" and "Wind Me Up," and was inducted into the Rock and Roll Hall of Fame as a member of Parliament-Funkadelic in 1997. Maceo Parker and Fred Wesley would eventually join Clinton's funk fest as members of the P-Funk horn section, the Horny Horns, and enjoy musical fun and freedom that they never experienced with Soul Brother No. 1.

While there was no denying the excitement of Mr. Dynamite's dance tunes, including "I Got the Feelin'" and the frenetic "Night Train," fans at the Uptown waited anxiously for his dramatic rendition of "Please, Please, Please," written by Bobby Byrd, Brown's frequent collaborator and a member of his background vocal group, the Famous Flames. Byrd's robust baritone can be heard on hits such as "Sex Machine," "Get Up, Get Into It, Get Involved" and "I Know You Got Soul" and "Soul Power."

Set to an undulating rhythm, Brown begged for forgiveness for his latest transgression, while professing his love for a female who is obviously hell-bent on making him "work for it."

With his plea apparently falling on deaf ears, Brown would scream in agony, spin around like a cyclone, then suddenly collapse to the floor on his knees as he clutched his microphone. To ease his suffering, the Famous Flames and Bobby Byrd would come over and drape a cape over the bereft Brown's broad shoulders, gently console him and help him to his feet.

With his head bowed in anguish, the spurned lover would begin to make his way off stage (undoubtedly inspecting patent leather shoes along the way) rhythmically chanting, "I . . . I . . . I . . . I." Suddenly, Brown, overcome with grief, would go into convulsions, throw the cape off and start running in place to the drummers rapid-fire rim shots like a man possessed before hitting his knees again and squealing at the top of his lungs. With the crowd going crazy, his faithful minions would come to his aid once more and the emotionally-charged scenario would repeat itself until Brown was dripping with sweat and the entire audience was going insane. But through it all, his well-processed pompadour never moved. Meanwhile, somewhere in the universe, possibly from the wings of that very same stage, a little boy was watching . . .

It's March 19, 2001, and I'm in the crowded pressroom at the Waldorf Astoria in New York City, along with members of the international media and a battalion of TV cameras and photographers from around the world. Sure, I'd covered many events in the Big Apple including film junkets and the Essence Awards, but on this particular night, there was a different kind of energy and excitement in the air. On this night, the one and only Michael Jackson would be inducted into the Rock and Roll Hall of Fame—for the second time.

In 1997, Sigmund Esco (Jackie), Toriano Adaryll (Tito), Jermaine La Jaune, Marlon David and Michael Joseph, five supremely talented brothers from Gary, Ind., were inducted into the prestigious Hall of Fame as the Jackson Five. However on this night, Michael, who had amassed 13 Grammys, 13 No. 1 singles and 32 gold and platinum records, and had made history with "Thriller," the best-selling album of all time, was about to be inducted as a solo artist, and the whole world came to witness and record the auspicious occasion.

Also among the inductees of the impressive Class of 2001 were performers Aerosmith, Solomon Burke, The Flamingos, Queen, Paul Simon, Steely Dan, Ritchie Valens, "sidemen" Johnnie Johnson and James Burton, and Chris Blackwell, founder of Island Records and the music mogul who is credited with making the legendary Bob Marley a global phenomenon.

My personal "Michael Moment" came when the self-anointed "King of Pop" finally arrived in the pressroom for the routine Q&A/photo session that takes place after each honoree is inducted. At one point, word began to spread that Jackson would not be coming to the pressroom, but when those in "power" realized that we were very serious about breaking up the place if MJ didn't show (remember, most of these people had come from halfway across the globe just to see HIM), that kind of crazy talk was quickly squashed. A compromise was reached in that Jackson could be photographed, but no questions would be permitted. I didn't care. I just wanted to see The Man—up close and personal.

My patience was rewarded. About an hour later, Jackson, accompanied by red-hot "boy band" (I hate that term) N'Sync, who had served as his presenters, entered the room. OOOOH! He was absolutely resplendent in a cream colored suit with gold accessories, and his hair was bouncin' and behavin'. Speaking of hair, Justin Timberlake, who up to that point was known for his curly locks, had unexpectedly cut them off. As he walked by, I said, "Justin! You cut your hair! It looks great!" With a smile he said,

"Thanks. I'm getting mixed reviews," and every scribe in the room began scribbling furiously.

Now imagine, if you can, a seasoned, award-winning journalist instantly reverting back to a star-struck seventh grader. In a voice that sounded nothing like my own assertive, full-bodied soprano, I said, "You look nice, Michael." Then, imagine my astonishment when Jackson, who was standing on a low platform about 10 feet away, looked me right at me at said, "Thank you." It's a good thing that they weren't allowing questions, because that was it for me. They were the only two words that he would utter the entire session, which ended abruptly when the idiot next to me broke the "no questions" rule and asked, "Michael! When's your album coming out?" in reference to "Invincible," Jackson's final studio album, and with that, the King of Pop was immediately whisked out of the room.

The only other moment that comes close was at the Four Seasons in Los Angeles when LL Cool J and I made eye contact and smiled at each other across a crowded room . . . but I digress. Enough about me—the consummate professional.

Long before that exciting evening in New York, years before MTV, years before "Thriller," "Billie Jean," the Elephant Man's bones, the hyperbaric chamber, and the child molestation allegations—even before their Motown debut "I Want You Back," was released, the Jackson Five, featuring a child prodigy named Michael, played the chitlin' circuit, using every opportunity to develop their showmanship and hone Michael's now legendary "chops."

"Prior to Motown, we were out doing the Apollo, the Uptown and other places four or five years before Motown," Marlon Jackson said in May 2012, just before embarking on The Jacksons' "Unity" reunion tour. "We started from the beginning. You started from the ground up and along the way, James Brown, Jackie Wilson, Joe Tex, all these people you see on the sidelines—Little Dion, you watch them perform and you pick up on things, and you see how they do things. Then you incorporate that type of stuff into your show, back in the day, and then you learn what moves people, what [doesn't] move people, how to structure a show, how to take them up and down—keep your audience captivated and take them on a journey."

Known even then as the cool and quiet one, Marlon remains just as unflappable today, stating that while playing the chitlin' circuit was a learning experience, a certain amount of prestige came with performing at East Coast venues such as the Uptown and the Apollo.

"It was always the same to me, because we looked at it as the East Coast audience, and they were always great," he said. "We didn't look forward to playing the Apollo as opposed to the Uptown. We looked forward to playing the East Coast, and going to the Apollo and going to the Uptown. That's the way we looked at it."

Everyone now pretty much acknowledges that producer Bobby Taylor, formerly of Bobby Taylor and the Vancouvers (not Diana Ross), is responsible for bringing the Jackson Five to Motown. That indeed, is true, but there is someone who was equally instrumental in their "discovery." Philadelphia music pioneer Weldon Mc Dougal, whose numerous accomplishments have largely gone unheralded, has memories of the Jackson Five that go even deeper, and add a little known dimension to the story, as well as an interesting Philly connection.

The brash and irreverent Mc Dougal, who, like comedians Bill Cosby and Dap Sugar Willie, was raised in North Philadelphia's Richard Allen Homes, was the City's first Black record promotions man. He also spent eight years working as Promotions Director, and Director of Special Projects for Motown Records, and also acted as a chaperone for the Jackson Five during their early days at Motown.

"I was Director of Special Projects, and whenever our artists would go somewhere, I would make it a point to make arrangements for the disc jockeys to come to that affair," Mc Dougal said during an exclusive interview. "So I would go to the affair ahead of time and pick out the VIP seating that I wanted.

"It just so happened that Bobby Taylor and the Vancouvers, for the first time, were playing in Chicago, so I went to the High Chaparral to make arrangements for the VIP seats. The manager was named Clarence. So I went in to talk to Clarence and he explained to me that I could have the tables. I also remember that while we were in there talking, it was Wednesday, which was when they had the talent shows. It was pretty crowded, but not that many people. [Clarence] was saying, 'Hey man, the people who win our talent show play on Friday, Saturday and Sunday with the main artist. They got some guys here named the Jackson Five. They always win.'

"So when I went into the main room, they were on, and they were doing 'Please, Please, Please' by James Brown. The audience, the little bit that was there, was going nuts! So they did real well.

"Meanwhile, while I'm standing in the wings, Joe Jackson came over to me and said, 'Hey man, I hear you're with Motown, and we would like to be on the Motown label.' I said, 'Well, I don't have nothing to do with putting anybody on the label. I'm the promotions man.' Then he said, 'Is there anything I can do to talk to anybody?' Then I thought of Bobby Taylor, who told me he had a production deal with Motown. That meant that he could produce anybody, and they would be interested in listening."

Mc Dougal says that at that point, he offered to introduce Joe Jackson to Bobby Taylor, who would be playing the High Chaparral that following Friday.

"When Joe Jackson came into the club that Friday night, he was with a guy from Steeltown Records," Mc Dougal continued. "The guy from Steeltown Records gave me about three records. I forgot what I did with them, but it was the records that they had recorded on the Jackson Five before that. I introduced them at that time to Bobby Taylor and Bobby Taylor liked them. The next thing I knew Bobby had signed [The Jackson Five] up, and they were on the road with Bobby Taylor."

"Weldon McDougal! Yes, I know him very well!" Marlon said. "He passed though, didn't he?" Indeed, the beloved music man who was such a valuable source for so many of my articles during the short time that I knew him, passed away in October 2010, but not before he explained to me, in great detail, how he had a hand in bringing the Jackson Five to the Uptown for the very first time.

"The next time I seen the Jackson Five, by the way, was at the Apollo," McDougal said. "I knew Bobby Taylor was going to be there, so I went there to see Bobby Taylor, and again, I made any kind of arrangements I could with the disc jockeys to get free tickets for them or their families or whatever.

Anyway, when I got there, I was just shocked to see all these kids at the back door. They had to go through like a little entourage, and they was hollerin' at Michael Jackson. I said, Hey man! What are you doin' here? He said, 'We sang, man! We sang, and we got over good!' I said, 'I see! I noticed!'

"And then we went to the dressing room and was just talking, and I want everybody to know this. Bobby Taylor was promotin' them guys to death! I mean, as much as he could, with his group. Anytime they would play somewhere, Bobby Taylor would try to get them on the gig.

"So what happened was, Bobby said, 'Man, we're going to the Uptown,' after they left the Apollo, and he said, 'Could you call George and see if he would use the guys?' So I called Georgie Woods right back there and I said, 'Hey man! They are killin' 'em! The people are goin' nuts!' He said, 'Who's their manager?' I said, 'It's their father, Joe.' So I got Joe and put him on the phone, and they came to the Uptown. That's the first and only time they ever came to the Uptown. That's how I got 'em there."

Stating that the J-5's impromptu engagement may have lasted only a weekend rather than the usual seven to ten days, Sam Reed who conducted his orchestra as they accompanied the group, recalled their show-stopping Uptown debut saying, "The people liked them, of course, because they appeared at the Apollo before they came to the Uptown. When they came to the Uptown, the Five Stairsteps were headliners, so the Five Stairsteps had more popularity than the Jackson Five at that time."

Marlon, who appears to be the most level-headed of the Jackson brothers, did not find competing with groups such as Chicago's Five Stairsteps, who had already charted with hits such as "You Waited Too Long," "Come Back" and "World of Fantasy" to be particularly intimidating and said, "I think at first it probably was, but after a while, when we kept winning the talent shows and things, we just did what we knew how to do and didn't think about it, to be honest with you. We realized that we were rockin' 'em!"

While he was very young at the time, Marlon does recall his experience at the Uptown Theater, before the J-5 exploded into superstar status. "I think the Emotions were on that show [and] the O'Jays," he said. "There was a group called Skip Sonny and the Pace Brothers—they were on that show, the Five Stairsteps were on that show. We used to all do the Apollo and the Uptown because Georgie Woods and Jimmy Bishop used to book those shows at the Uptown."

Indeed the O'Jays were on the bill with the J-5, as were the Manhattans, and Blue Lovett has vivid memories of his first encounter with the now legendary musical family—particularly their precocious lead singer. "Michael was so dynamic with dancing like James Brown and throwing the microphone!" Lovett said. "At that time, they didn't have their own record out. They were doing other artists' stuff, and the "First Family of Soul" at that time was the Five Stairsteps, and Michael & Company came and snatched the rug from under them!"

The candid and comical Eddie Levert concurred saying, "I remember the first time when we played the Uptown and Michael Jackson and the Jackson Five were there. They opened the show, and these boys, the

Hesitations had to follow them. And they had no record at this time. They was doin' that 'Who's Lovin' You'—their version of it, before they even recorded it. They was doin' 'Stand' by Sly & the Family Stone, and they was killin' the crowd. The kids was goin' crazy! By the time the Hesitations were coming on, they were still talkin' about 'More! More! More!' The Hesitations were going into 'Born Free,' and that would be the end of them. 'Get off the stage!'"

"I wrote that song many, many years ago," Smokey Robinson said of his original composition, "Who's Lovin' You." "It was kind of like a hit for the Miracles. That song's about somebody who had somebody who really loved them, but they didn't appreciate it, and they did the person wrong. They did them so wrong that the person finally ended up hating them, and then they started to regret it. They wanted that person back. They wanted to know where that person was and who they were with.

"It is absolutely impossible for an 11 year-old boy to know what that song is talking about, but [Michael Jackson] sang it. He sang like he wrote it. He sang so good until when we'd play that song live in our concerts, young people would come up and say, 'Why are you singing his song?'"

Leon Huff, who along with Kenny Gamble, would cut two albums on the Jacksons several years later, was also at the Uptown for those performances and recalled, "They were great! Michael Jackson was such a dynamic talent! The Five Stairsteps were good too, for what they were doing, but the Jackson Five were another thing because Michael Jackson was singing like an adult when he was nine years old. If you go back to his story, and listen to Michael at nine years old—that's a tape. They filmed it. Listen to him singing 'Climb Every Mountain' and 'I Saw Mommy Kissing Santa Claus' at nine years old. This boy didn't hit no flat notes at all, so they can leave Michael alone when it comes to singin'!"

Lovett recalled that offstage, Michael and his brothers were just like any other All-American boys saying, "We took Michael backstage with Marlon, and he was out there wrestling and hangin' out with the little hometown kids backstage."

"When he first came to Philadelphia, I remember we were backstage at the Uptown Theater, and Michael just wanted to go next door and get some soul food from Pearl's," said Philadelphia radio legend Joe "Butterball" Tamburro. "We used to go right out the back street, go to the next building, and she had a little thing in her kitchen. She'd cook and we all ate there. He loved to go there and get some soul food and just hang out with the guys."

Throughout Jackson's spectacular career, the lessons that he learned through playing the chitlin'circuit with legendary entertainers such as James Brown and Jackie Wilson remained in evidence.

When "I Want You Back," hit the airwaves in January 1970, it was a joyous fanfare announcing the official debut of the J5 and introducing their exclusive new groove, which would be christened "bubblegum soul." With a passion and deep regret that was well beyond his 11 years, Michael, in his pre-pubescent boy soprano remorsefully admitted:

When I had you to myself,
I didn't want you around.
Those pretty faces always made you stand out in a crowd.
But someone picked you from the bunch.
Once glance was all it took.
Now it's much too late for me to take a second look.

A cavalcade of hits, written and produced by The Corporation (Berry Gordy, Freddie Perren, Alphonso "Fonce" Mizell and Deke Richards) would follow, including "ABC," "The Love You Save" and "I'll Be There," all reaching Number One in 1970.

Michael Jackson was groomed as a solo artist while still a member of the J-5, and in October 1971, at age 13, he released the first in a successful string of solo singles over the next year that included "Got to Be There" and "Rockin' Robin" as well as "Ben," his poignant ode to a rat which reached Number One on the charts.

Jermaine shocked the world (and broke my heart) when he married Hazel Gordy, the boss' daughter in 1973, making things a bit messy when the group decided to leave Motown. He opted to stay, embarking on a mildly successful solo career, and was replaced by youngest brother, Stephen Randall, a.k.a. Randy. Changing their name to The Jacksons, the group signed with Epic Records in 1976.

Renewing the Philly connection that they had forged over the years, the Jacksons released two albums produced by Gamble and Huff, including "The Jacksons" (1976) and "Goin' Places" (1977). Under their tutelage, the brothers would enjoy a new-found creative freedom that was forbidden at Motown.

"What happened was that I knew the Jacksons since they were little kids playing the Uptown," Gamble explained. "They used to come by my house, and their father and all of them. We used to make dinner for them and all that kind of stuff when they were here in town—when they were very young. So we maintained that relationship with them over the years.

"One of the things that drew us together was that my family was Jehovah's Witnesses, and so was their family, so Katherine Jackson and my mother and all of them, they kind of blended together. We had a lot to talk about.

"When they were leaving Motown, I was talking to their father, Joe Jackson, and they really wanted to come to Philly International. We were doing very good during that time, so I was trying to encourage them to come to Philly International. Of course, we were being distributed by CBS and Epic at that particular time, and were doing very well with them. So I called the people at Epic and I told them. I said, 'Listen. I'm trying to sign the Jacksons,' and they said, 'Well, we're trying to sign them, too!' So it's like a little mouse trying to compete with a big, giant elephant, 'cause we couldn't offer them nowhere close to what these people were offering them. So I told Joe Jackson, 'Joe, they're offering you cartoons'—'cause this is CBS, you know? 'They're offering you all kinds of incentives. Maybe there's some way to work it out.' So I talked to the president of Epic Records, at that time. His name was Ron Luxemburg.

"So Ron and I were very close, and he said, 'Well, look. Can you and Huff record their first album?' Generally, during that time, I did not record people who were not on Philadelphia International Records, 'cause people were calling me from everywhere. 'Would you do a cut on Gladys Knight?' 'Would you do a cut on this person and that person?' I said, 'No,' because we had been through that phase as independent producers Huff and I, and what happens is, you get a hit on somebody—like Wilson Pickett. We got a big hit on Wilson Pickett—'Don't Let the Green Grass Fool You.' So then when you get the big album—we got a gold record with him—the next album, they decided to use someone else. So I said, 'We can't do that after we put all our energy into it. So that's when we started to form Philly International, so we could develop our own artists.

"Plus, the Jacksons are special. So I talked to Huff and I said, 'Okay, we'll do it, but let's do it like a joint label.' So you'll notice on those records with the Jacksons, you've got the Philadelphia International logo, and the Epic logo, which helped them an awful lot too, 'cause most of the Black radio people thought that this giant, CBS, was trying to take the Jacksons from Motown. That was floatin' around. So we had a good relationship with everybody, and that's how they were able to be here in Philadelphia. The rest is all history."

Once the deal was done, Gamble & Huff would encourage the Jacksons, Michael in particular, to tap into a creativity that was yet to be discovered.

"At our first meeting when they came to our offices here at 309, we talked about how we would work together, and some of their desires, because we were really busy," said Gamble. "We had the O'Jays, we had Harold Melvin & the Blue Notes, we had Patti La Belle . . . we had all these artists, and we still were recording all of them. This was like a machine, 'cause it wasn't just Gamble and Huff. If you look on the Jacksons' album, you had Dexter Wansel, who did a couple of sides, you had McFadden & Whitehead, who did a couple of sides, and I tried to get Thom Bell to work with us, but he was so busy! He was working with the Spinners, he was working with Elton John . . .

"So Michael, at that meeting, and Tito, who I thought was an excellent musician, they were interested in doing a more adult kind of music, 'cause their music with Motown, all of it basically sounded kind of like, the same—like pop/bubblegum music, a little bit. Except for 'Never Can Say Goodbye' which was a fantastic song.

"So how do you compete with Motown? That, to me, was the ultimate in record companies! Motown inspired us, and I don't think there would probably even be a lot of Black record companies today if it had not been for Motown. We used the Motown blueprint, and that blueprint was that you get a lot of great songwriters, they become producers, and you put teams of people together, and you all compete against each other. Like when the O'Jays came in. All these writers would be writing for the O'Jays, and then you pick the best songs from each writer. And the same thing happened with the Jacksons.

"At our meeting with the Jacksons, we discussed a few things, and we told them, 'Give us about six weeks then come back. We're going to put the machine to work.' So everybody started writing songs for the Jacksons. Huff and I must have written about 12 songs. McFadden & "Whitehead wrote about 10 or 12 songs, and then Dexter had about a half dozen songs, so by the time they came back, there was like 35 songs, and I told them, 'You also write some songs,' because they had mentioned that they wanted to start writing and producing themselves, and I said, 'Well, let's do it!' Because I encouraged people. I always thought that Huff and I could stand the competition. We had to be strong, so me and Huff, we encouraged young writers to become producers and get off on their own, and look at the business as a business."

"I can remember writing songs for them, and the songs that Huff and I were writing for them were songs like 'Let Me Show You the Way to Go' and 'Enjoy Yourself,' and another song that we had, and Michael loved it. It was called 'Man of War.' 'Man of War' was one of his favorite songs, 'cause our whole thing was messages—message in the music, and that's what Michael wanted to do. He said, 'Man, I want to do some messages!'"

In later years, that desire would ultimately manifest itself in such inspirational anthems as "Heal the World," "Earth Song," and the classic "We Are the World," co-written with Lionel Richie. However, it was with the light-hearted love song "Blues Away" that Michael took his first tentative but promising steps as a producer/songwriter.

"That was Michael's song," Gamble said. "Michael wrote that song, and I think McFadden & Whitehead and myself. He needed help with it, so we all got in the studio with him, 'cause he played the piano a little bit. So he played the song on the piano, and he was telling me how he wanted it to go, I said, 'Well, you do it.' So I left the studio and let him do it so that way, he could produce his own, and he did an excellent job!

"I came back in when he started to overdub his voice—when he put his voice on, and he had all of these great ideas about how to record his voice—like doubling his voice, doing all kinds of little ad libs and whatever.

> *I'd like to be yours tomorrow*
> *So I'm giving you some time*
> *To think it over today*
> *But you can't chase my blues away*
> *No matter what you say.*

"He had it all thought out in his head," Gamble said. "As a matter of fact, they had two songs on each album. They had 'Blues Away' and 'You've Got to Change Your Style of Life.' Michael wrote 'Blues Away' by himself, and 'You've Got to Change Your Style of Life,' all the brothers, they wrote it together.

"So they all were participating, and the conclusion that I came up with after listening to them, I told Michael and Tito and all of the rest of them, 'You guys need to express yourselves. You need to produce yourselves, and whatever I can do to help y'all, I'll help you.' They were extremely talented, and I also told Ron Luxemburg from Epic, 'These guys need to produce themselves,' because they had a sound in their heads. And then the first album that they produced on themselves was 'Destiny,' but the song that was in it was 'Shake Your Body Down to the Ground,' and I said, 'Man! These jokers is rollin'!' Because their whole thing was dancin'! It was a great experience, and Michael used to thank me all the time for showing him how to put his songs together."

"It was a wonderful experience!" said Huff. Michael said that we changed his whole work ethic, because when he was at Motown he was much younger, and he didn't have that work ethic that we had because he had a curfew. By the time that he grew up and got to us, that changed when he came to Philly because we taught Michael that you create as long as you can. So when he came to Philly, the first time we was in the studio, they were supposed to stop at 10:00. They stopped at 10:00, but Michael didn't like it 'cause me and Gamble was just getting' started at 10:00 sometimes. You know, creativity, ain't no time limit on it! "But Michael loved it, staying up all night, because that's when those juices was flowin'!"

"The 2 albums that we did with them probably was the most turbulent times of their career, because Jermaine had left, they were not working—they were trying to get themselves back together again," Gamble recalled. "They were facing all kinds of backlash from the industry, especially from radio, because a lot of the Black radio people thought that CBS was trying to take advantage of a Black record company."

Since Gamble and Huff insisted on rehearsals during the recording process, Philly became a temporary home for the Jacksons, who took up residence at the Latham Hotel at 17th & Chestnut Streets while they worked on their new music. While Gamble maintained that Michael "stayed focused" in the studio, his occasional outings in Center City Philadelphia were a foretaste of things to come.

"This is the only artist out of all the years that we've been here in the city that when people found out that they were here, you had drill teams and fan clubs outside the building!" said Gamble. "I used to look outside my office window and it might be 60 young girls down there waiting for them to come out. But that shows you what kind of an impact this family has had all of these years.

"I can remember one day that Michael wanted to get some new sneaks, so we walked around Chestnut Street, and while we was walking around Chestnut Street everything was cool, so we went to the sneaker place. By the time we were in that sneaker store for about 15 minutes, we looked out the window. There must have been 200 people standing outside—like a flash mob—just waiting for him to come out. He said, 'Mr. Gamble, what are we gonna do?' I said, 'We're gonna walk back to the office.' The security were there. But it was cool. I said, 'Don't worry about it,' 'cause they were just hollerin' and screamin' 'Michael! Michael!'"

The world would catch a glimpse of Michael's brilliance in 1978, when he co-starred with his mentor, Diana Ross, in a film adaptation of the Tony Award-winning musical, "The Wiz." It was in this production, in which he danced, sang and frolicked his way through an urban Oz as Scarecrow that Michael would meet legendary jazz man Quincy Jones, who served as the film's musical supervisor and music producer. Jones would become the producer of Michael's best-known albums and the first of these, the dynamic "Off the Wall," released in 1979 and featuring the tunes "Don't Stop 'Til You Get Enough and "Rock With You," would introduce Michael Jackson as a confident and creative 21 year-old artist. However, it was with the release of "Thriller" in November of 1982 that the magic and the madness of "Michaelmania" would truly take hold.

In June 2009, beloved WDAS radio icon Butterball, who had been a valued and reliable source for many of my articles, was hospitalized due to a prolonged illness. Yet, with the news of Michael Jackson's sudden death on June 25, 2009, he took the time to reflect on his association with the legendary entertainer, and share with me the story of how he was the first to play "Thriller," which would become the best-selling album of all-time, in the Philadelphia market, gleefully adding that he did so without permission of Jackson's label, Epic Records . . .

"Butter" giggled like a child who had gotten into some mischief as he recounted his courageous coup, and explained, "The 'Thriller' album was getting ready to come out, and we were always in a radio war trying to beat the other stations down and they tried to beat us down. I remember I got a phone call that somebody could get me a copy of the 'Thriller' album from the plant, which was top secret—you couldn't get near there. I'll never forget. I went at like, 5:00 in the afternoon and I met this person and got a copy of 'Thriller,' went back to the radio station and started playing it, and I played it all night that night! [One time] after another, after another—I had the whole city going crazy! The following morning I got a 'cease and desist' from Epic Records that I had to stop playing it, but I had already done it—I didn't care! But it was one of the most exciting moments, to have that and nobody else had it! And at that moment, he was on fire!" Sadly, Joseph "Butterball" Tamburro passed away on July 27, 2012.

"Thriller," which set off a firestorm of triumph, turmoil and tragedy that no one could have predicted was followed by the 1987 release "Bad," which featured the hits "The Way You Make Me Feel," "Smooth Criminal" and "Dirty Diana" as well as the title track, and Jackson, the ultimate perfectionist, reportedly felt immense pressure to top himself.

"He didn't let that stop him," said Spike Lee, who directed the video for Jackson's anthem, "They Don't Care About Us." "He wanted "Bad" to sell 100 million copies. He wanted to top himself every time he came out."

As of 2012, "Bad" had sold over 45 million units, and at the 69th Venice International Film Festival, Lee premiered his documentary, "Bad 25," which chronicles the making of the album and commemorates the 25th anniversary of its release on August 31, 1987. On Thanksgiving Day 2012, the film premiered on network television, airing on ABC.

Shortly after the release of "Bad," Jackson's well-documented personal problems began, causing media attention to turn from his artistic excellence to his amusing eccentricities and eventually ugly allegations.

There was his over-the-top Neverland Ranch, which featured a menagerie of exotic animals and a full-fledged amusement park, his quest to acquire the Elephant Man's bones, his laundry list of plastic surgeries, his highly publicized financial difficulties and his penchant for sleeping in a hyperbaric chamber (which eventually turned out not to be such a crazy notion after all). However, the bizarre behavior that inspired the British tabloids to label him "Wacko Jacko" turned serious when on two separate occasions, he was accused of child molestation—allegations that Jackson vehemently and steadfastly denied.

On Sept. 15, 1993, lawyers for a 13-year-old filed a civil suit against Jackson for seduction and sexual abuse. On Dec. 22, Jackson responded to the allegations via satellite from his Neverland Ranch saying, "I am totally innocent of any wrongdoing." On Jan. 25, 1994, he settled with his accuser out of court for an undisclosed sum estimated at $20 million.

Eleven years later, on June 13, 2005, Jackson was found not guilty in a California court for a second charge of molestation leveled by 13-year-old Gavin Arvizo. Jackson would eventually leave Neverland Ranch, vowing never to return.

Gamble, who stayed in contact with Jackson throughout the years, reflected on the trials that beset the legendary superstar saying, "I've always maintained a good relationship with Michael. As a matter of fact, the last time I saw Michael Jackson was maybe a couple of years before he passed—around the time he was going through all those trials. So he had called me up and I met him in New York and he wanted to tell me. He said, 'Gamble, you *know* me. I would *never* do anything like that!' I said, "I believe you, but you've got yourself in a situation,' and I said, 'You've got to get away from these people!' That was my advice. But who knows how life is when you're that kind of a star? When you can't move without people pulling at you all the time?

"We used to talk about everything. We used to talk about spiritual things. He was very, very spiritual, and he was talking about all the things that he wanted to do. He really meant that he wanted to heal the world. He really wanted to help out, and so on that level, he and I were kind of on the same page about wanting to help people."

As his mood grew increasingly somber, Gamble recalled the last time he saw Michael Jackson. "The day I saw him, I made him laugh 'cause we talked about all the old times, but he seemed like he was . . . when I think back on it now, I wish I would have asserted myself a little bit more to get with him," he said introspectively. "As a matter of fact, Huff and I were in Califormia for the Billboard Icon Awards, and a girl that used to work with him, her name is Raymone Bain, she called me and she said, 'Gamble, go by and see Michael. He needs some help. He needs a friend.' So I . . . boy . . ."

As Gamble's voice trailed off, I asked, "So did you not go?" "No, I didn't go, and I feel bad that I didn't go," he responded. "I said to myself when we were in the car, 'He got all them bodyguards and stuff. They're not going to let me get close to him.' But now that I think about it, I should have asserted myself and went there. You never know what would have happened, but that's what I thought about when I found out he had passed, 'cause I really feel as though he needed a friend."

Michael Jackson, who often felt like an unwelcome stranger in his own country, lived overseas for much of the latter part of his life, choosing to settle in exotic locales such as Bahrain and Berlin. On March 5, 2009, after years away from the spotlight, Jackson held a splashy press conference in London to announce a comeback of sorts. Stating that he would be appearing in a series of spectacular concerts at London's O2 Arena, he vowed that they would be his last live performances. "These will be my final shows, my final performances—in London," Jackson said. "This is it. And when I say, 'This is it,' I really mean this is it. This is the final curtain call." The production was dubbed "This Is It," which in hindsight was ominous, if not prophetic.

On June 25, 2009, Michael Jackson, age 50, died suddenly at his rented home in Los Angeles from an overdose of Propofol, a powerful anesthetic designated specifically for use in hospitals. The lethal dosage was administered by Jackson's personal physician, Dr. Conrad Murray, who in 2011 was convicted of involuntary manslaughter and sentenced to four years in prison. Reportedly, he is serving his term at the L.A. County Jail instead of a state prison because of California's "realignment" process, which places non-violent felons in local jails due to overcrowding.

In the aftermath of Jackson's shocking and tragic death, an impromptu memorial service was held in front of the Uptown Theater, where his extraordinary career began.

"It was Quincy Jones who brought Michael to his epitome—to where Michael wanted to be, but I'm just glad I was part of the growth," said Huff. Gamble added, "It's very seldom that you find a young 12, 13 year-old boy that can sing like that. I mean, he had a tremendous voice—this was no kiddie game! This was real singing, and he often gave credit to James Brown and to Smokey Robinson. These are the people that he studied. He studied those people and incorporated all that stuff into himself. He just had something special."

"Michael Jackson was my brother," said Robinson, one of the people who knew him best. "Michael Jackson changed the face of music—changed the look of music. I'm a music collector. I have the first videos of people like Bessie Smith, Cab Calloway and Count Basie. Michael Jackson, from the overall picture of it—the singing, the dancing and all of that—was the best I have ever seen! He started a whole new era!"

10

What Happened To The Music?

AS THE '60S faded into history, change was definitely in the air. The R&B shows at the Uptown weren't as frequent, and the lines on North Broad Street weren't nearly as long. For the first time, a tradition that began in 1958 was in jeopardy.

"George and them started doing less shows. I guess the groups were asking for so much money," Sam Reed said. "Things got sky high. I remember the last show I did there was James Brown, because you know, James Brown always drew a crowd. And then the next one, he tried the Philadelphia thing—the Delfonics, the Intruders—all groups here in Philadelphia. He tried that and it was OK, but the crowds weren't as large as they used to be when the Motown acts were coming through." So, what happened to the music?

Actually, a number of factors contributed to the demise of Georgie Woods' R&B shows at the Uptown, and ultimately, the theater itself. As society began to change, so did the atmosphere and circumstances that once made the Uptown essential to the Black music industry. The end of segregation opened up opportunities for Black artists to play larger "mainstream" venues such as The Spectrum, Philly's state-of-the-art multi-purpose arena, as well as major showrooms in Atlantic City and Las Vegas. The area immediately surrounding the theater also changed dramatically, with escalating gang violence and increased drug activity making a trip to the Uptown downright dangerous.

There were also major changes to the music industry at large. Now "crossing over" to pop (white) radio, Black acts, no longer depending on the once-powerful Georgie Woods to decide their fate, charged more and more money for their services.

Disco was also on the rise, with its robotic beat, non-descript vocals and highly produced "tracks" making traditional R&B sound passé, and forcing Black acts that did not crossover off the air completely. Theaters like the Uptown soon gave way to glitzy and lucrative discotheques such as Studio 54, The Library, Club Impulse and Emerald City. "Financially, it wasn't feasible anymore," said Woods, who was forced to pull the plug on his once-popular concert series in 1972. The Uptown eventually closed its doors in 1978.

The elements, vandalism and years of neglect took their toll on the grand old movie house, and with the Uptown no longer driving the local economy, once-thriving businesses that depended on the theater for their customers and clients were also forced to close, sending the entire community into a deep decline.

"It appeared that the Uptown would have new life, when in 1980, the building was reopened by prominent community activist John Bowser and his son Kyle, under the name New Uptown Theater and Entertainment Center (NUTEC). "He had grand plans to restore that facility and bring it back to what we remember from the '60s and '70s," Kyle said of his father. They operated NUTEC together until John Bowser's death in 1983, and the legendary venue went dark once more.

Former Uptown bandleader Leon Mitchell recalled, "John Bowser and his family tried to bring it back with the NUTEC Uptown, which was a great idea. I think he was kind of nuts, but what he tried to do was kind of funny. He figured if he could get 1,000 members to become "friends" of the Uptown that he could assign a seat to each one of those members in the theater, and then whenever they came to see a show, they would have to sit in their seat. But what happened was, when they would put a show on that people want to come to see, they wasn't going to sit way in the back of the theater when their seat was in the back of the theater, but wasn't nobody in the seats down front.

"I first talked to him about it when they were trying to open the theater back up. I said, 'John, that's not going to work. The only thing that you can do to make that work is have advance notice to your members so that they can come and get the seat first before anybody else even hears about the show coming. So they tried to do that later on, but it was too late then.

"Then John died and his kids tried to keep it going, but they had a nice thing going with the clubs up over the theater. They opened a small club where you could put an organ trio in, and over that was a full-fledged disco, and over that was the Copasetic Lounge, which was like an upscale supper club on the fourth floor. That did pretty good until WDAS got involved with the disco, and all of the drug use and everybody started coming in on Saturday night, and I think the second week they had it, somebody got shot, and that was the end of that."

"I was there when John was doing that, and I told him not to do it, because he didn't have any parking. That's the first thing," said Kenny Gamble. "The second thing was trying to do too many things with that building. He tried to put clubs upstairs and all of that—he said he was going to do it anyway. I did support him, even though I thought that the business had changed.

"What the Uptown did was develop artists. They did five, six shows a day for 10 days. How many people is that (in the audience)? But the thing of it is that they started to play bigger venues, like the Spectrum. Now the Spectrum was controlled by Electric Factory (Concerts) and all those people, so there was a conflict with the Black promoters, 'cause Georgie Woods was a Black promoter, and how do you get into the Spectrum and all these other places when they had deals with the white promoters? So there was always a conflict, and sometimes they worked it out, and sometimes they didn't, because if you were the Temptations, and somebody said, 'I'm going to give you $5 to play the Uptown, but you're going to be there for 10 days, and you've got to do five shows a day.' Then somebody comes to you and says, 'Well, I'm going to give you that same $5, but you've only got to work one night and do one show.'"

On Oct. 24, 1990, True Light Community Ministries purchased the Uptown Theater for $630,000. "I think what happened is an evangelist took it over—Reverend Somebody," said Sam Reed. "They said after he got through with it, it just went down. The building was destroyed. All the plumbing and all that kind of stuff wasn't kept up."

While the future of the historic Uptown Theater remains in question, its lasting impact on the Philadelphia community is unmistakable.

"The Uptown Theater was obviously a place we all loved to go see music," said Kevin Eubanks, who played in the neighborhood bands that populated Philly in the 70s, and was conducting jazz demonstrations and high school master classes on behalf of the Thelonius Monk Institute when we spoke in 2011.

"You're growing up and you're learning all these things, so it was another component of how music in your community does so much, which is why I go into the high schools and try and keep things energized and try and find better ways to introduce students to music and the disciplines, and the fun in music.

"And try to let them know this is not just a musical thing, it's a community thing. It's an education thing. It's not just music. It's the same as learning math, as learning English, and in some ways, even deeper than that. So just having the existence of music in your community does so much and touches so many people on so many different levels."

"The Uptown was kind of like a home away from home," said Jerry Butler. "I had lots of friends, and I don't mean just friends when they would come to the theater, I'm talking about friends that you went to their homes, you hung out with them, you played cards with them, you did the Philly cheesesteak thing—the whole nine yards. Then there was a whole group of athletes that used to come to the theater. We're going back to the days of Wilt Chamberlain, when Wilt Chamberlain was a rookie." As of August 2012, there was cautious optimism that the Uptown Theater could be restored to its original architectural splendor and return to its place of importance in the community.

The exterior of the Uptown Theater as it appeared on August 15, 2012. Photo: Abdul R. Sulayman

Linda Richardson, president of the Uptown Entertainment & Development Corporation. Photo: Abdul R. Sulayman

At a press conference held on August 15, 2012, Walter Gallas, left, field director for the Philadelphia Field Office of the National Trust for Historic Preservation, along with Linda Richardson, announce a $30,000.00 grant for the restoration of the Uptown Theater. Photo: Abdul R. Sulayman

"Uptown Reunion," a vibrant mural by Peter Pagast, adorns the exterior of the Uptown Theater. Photo: Abdul R. Sulayman

11

Back To The Future

AS I SAT on the hallowed stage of the Uptown Theater back in the summer of 2010, where just the night before, vandals had broken in and "tagged" the curtains with fresh graffiti, the woman sitting across from me was Linda Richardson, president of the Uptown Entertainment & Development Corporation (UEDC), the organization that now owns and is currently attempting to restore the building.

I met Richardson, a staunch community advocate, in 2009, when I interviewed her, along with her daughter Aissia Richardson and Earl Young for a fundraiser in support of the project, and she has been relentless in her efforts to revitalize the building. So just who is Linda Richardson, now a Burlington, N.J., resident, and how did she come to be entrusted with such a precious piece of Philadelphia history?

"I actually started as a dancer and an actress and was very interested in the Black Arts movement, but more particularly, just wanted to perform," Richardson explained. "So in the early days, before the height of civil rights, I was into trying to do something for the community and do something for the arts. So the community won out, but I still have a real appreciation for the arts.

"I was a modern dancer, and I studied at the Philadelphia Dance Academy, which was a precursor to the University of the Arts, which now has that program, and also studied with a theater group which used to meet in the basement of what is now Freedom Theatre.

"The night that Martin Luther King was assassinated, the actors were studying lines for a play, and we heard a lot of commotion and we found out that Martin Luther King was assassinated, and so we went out into the community. People were upset, and we thought that we could talk to them about art and hope and vision. So we talked to a lot of the people in the neighborhood and heard about some of their concerns and their aspirations, and from that point on I felt that art was more esoteric and not necessarily of value, although that was from a young person's standpoint. But I felt that I was much more needed in the community, so I pretty much decided to work as a community organizer."

Shortly thereafter, Richardson found a way to answer that calling. "I was looking for a job. I was a single mother, I had two children to raise, so I found out through my faith-based organization that there was a job for a community organizer," she explained. "I didn't know what that meant, but they were looking for someone and I interviewed anyway. It was a broad-based group of civil rights, anti-war organizations that were trying to do some domestic issues connected to the Vietnam War.

"And so I became a community organizer, met with community members, developed programs and found that I was really good at fundraising. I didn't even know that you could have a career in fundraising, but I was able to articulate to people who had money some of the [concerns of] people who didn't have money and who didn't have services. So that was what I did. I was able to raise money from large, wealthy people to support community issues."

Richardson turned her focus to the Uptown Theater when she became an integral part of the community surrounding it.

"In the 1990s, I was part of a project to renovate five townhouses across the street from the Uptown," she said. "That was completed in about 1995, and I moved my offices on the second floor of the building. Neighborhood people were complaining about the vandalism—people coming into the Uptown and vandalizing, so I called my City Council person, who was John Street, and his chief of staff was Darrell Clarke. He said, 'If you don't have keys you can't do anything. You have to own it.'"

Now firmly entrenched in the community, Richardson's ability to listen to the people and respond to their needs lead to the purchase of the Uptown.

"I talked to the community, and I was able to get a grant from the Governor's [Advisory] Commission of African American Affairs, and they provided a grant to do a feasibility study," she explained. The feasibility study was done under my direction. Actually, it was under the direction of then-entertainer Teddy Pendergrass, who expressed interest in the project, but at the end of the project he wanted to perform—continue doing his performing, and so I asked my Board of Directors if they would be interested in shepherding a project that would acquire the Uptown.

"And so, it became an economic development arm of the organization and then at some point, we decided to incorporate a separate entity, and so we incorporated the Uptown Entertainment & Development Corporation to finish the acquisition. The Uptown Entertainment & Development Corporarion is the owner. In 1995 we began the project, and the acquisition was finally completed in 2001."

Richardson ultimately became aware of the theater's sentimental value in the community and recalled, "I think like everyone, I knew about the Uptown, had a love for the Uptown. I never went during its heyday, but so many of my friends and relatives went to the Uptown, and so to see the building vacant was something that I was real concerned about. I thought that something should be done—particularly since I wanted to have the block be established as part of the Avenue of the Arts. Eventually it did become the Avenue of the Arts North, but there was no performing venues on this end of the Avenue of the Arts North, and I thought that the Uptown would be a great, great venue to be the anchor for that."

On Saturday, October 20, 2007, in a festive ceremony outside the theater, Mayor John Street presented a $1,000,000 grant to the Uptown Entertainment & Development Corporation for renovation of the historic theater and the creation of a new performing arts center on the Avenue of the Arts North. The ceremony unveiled the street signs of "Georgie Woods Boulevard," which includes the blocks of North Broad Street from York Street to Diamond Street, and also marked the dedication of the colorful mural that now adorns the building.

Executed by Peter Pagast for Philadelphia Mural Arts Program in 2006, the mural, titled "Uptown Reunion, "is a celebration of Philadelphia's legendary Uptown Theater and the artists who performed there."

While it has been an arduous process, Richardson and her daughter have been diligent in their effort to raise funds and keep public awareness focused on the project.

"The fundraising has been very difficult because we're in a very difficult time for everybody," Richardson said. "Arts and culture is also something that is not as valued as it could be, but we believe that art is food for the soul. So our fundraising effort is to link the preservation of the Uptown with some of the emerging needs that have occurred in the community. One—to be able to provide some jobs, two—to be able to provide youth entrepreneurship programs, and three—to be able to have a performing arts venue.

"The fundraising has been, first, looking at stabilizing, so we were able to raise $217,000.00 to stabilize the building, and then we were able to raise $2 million from the city and the state to begin the renovations and to put in some of the plumbing systems and to fix the roof, and some of the things that are not so sexy, but are necessary in development. We're hoping to raise the balance with our Capital Campaign." Richardson estimates that it will take approximately $8 million to complete the project.

The UEDC took a significant step forward on August 15, 2012, when the organization announced a $30,000.00 grant from the 1772 Foundation, which "provides funding to help preserve American historical treasures." According to Corbitt Banks, board chair of the UEDC, the grant has been designated for "Phase 2" of the restoration of the Uptown, which includes restoring the marquee and replacing the traditional lighting with bed lights, as well as renovating the box office with new doors, insulation and lighting. "This project will begin in early fall, and will be the first of many projects to restore the lobby, auditorium and balcony as part of Phase 2," Banks said.

In the fall of 2012, as I drive past the Uptown on my way to the newsroom each morning, the work appears to be underway. The building is fenced off, and since August, a trailer and Port-A-Potty have been sitting in front of it. Banners touting Allied Construction Services, Clearwater Concrete & Masonry and John Wieber, Inc. adorn the fence, and signage placed on the marquee invites business owners to lease space in the office building. Occasionally, there are sightings of men wearing hard hats, carrying what appear to be blueprints. Richardson has an ambitious plan for the future of the theater as well as the community-at-large, and explained it in great detail.

"Our organization is going to move in and occupy the sixth floor for our headquarters," she said. "I would like to be able to have the block the way it was, where there's people coming to go to restaurants and people standing in lines around the corner, but we certainly can't sell tickets for 50 cents the way it was done in the 50s.

"So I would like to see the building preserved. The building has deteriorated tremendously between the time we acquired it and the time we were able to raise the money. So we want to be able to keep it from deteriorating, because that's more expensive. The more it deteriorates, the more expensive it becomes.

"We would like to see the building as a way for young people to participate in the entertainment business, but offer young producers and promoters the opportunity to showcase some of their artists. We'd like to have an office space and maybe if somebody comes to town—say, a Wynton Marsalis—who may be playing downtown, they might want to have a place to stay, so we'll have a loft. So that's another thing we'd do. And this is part of a collective—not just me—but a collective vision to be able to make the Uptown the new era in entertainment . . . something that the next generation can participate in."

With regard to the next generation, for two semesters in 2011, I happily agreed to be a guest speaker at my alma mater, Temple University, for a course on the history of the Uptown Theater. My objective was to perpetuate the legend and the legacy of the theater by sharing it with a generation that had no idea of what the abandoned building just up the street from campus once meant to the community.

To make their Uptown experience more authentic, I asked Earl Young to join me, and he graciously agreed, bringing one of his two Grammys and a couple of his gold and platinum records with him. Literally a living history of the Philly Sound, with his musical contributions preceding even the creative collaboration of Gamble & Huff, Young shared his memories of playing on the Uptown stage with some of the finest musicians in the annals of jazz and R&B, as well as his vast knowledge of the music industry. By end of the session, the class, which included a baby boomer that obviously, had attended the shows at the Uptown, had a much greater appreciation of what the stately, but grossly neglected building at Broad and Dauphin means to Philadelphia's cultural landscape.

In the course of reporting on Philly's influential music scene, I have felt encouraged by a new generation of show biz professionals—all Philly natives—who also feel compelled to keep the Uptown legend alive.

"I'm in contact with the group that's trying to preserve the Uptown Theater," said Fatin Dantzler, one half of the husband and wife vocal duo, Kindred the Family Soul. "I, as a musician, have been very fortunate in assisting. Even though the Uptown has been closed for many years, I had the opportunity to perform there right before it closed up again the last time. In knowing the tradition—knowing the history of the place, I think that it is incumbent upon us to do everything in our power as a community of artists and as Philadelphians to try to get that place reinstated and reopened and refurbished. I think that it's very, very important.

"I would love to see that day, and any and everything that I can do to pledge my support and dedication to that cause, I'm going to do that, as

I told the committee as well. I look forward to working with them in the near future on whatever ideas that they have to try to make that a reality."

As the son of Lee Andrew Thompson, lead singer for Uptown topliners Lee Andrews & the Hearts, drummer and producer Ahmir "Questlove" Thompson of the Grammy Award-winning hip hop troupe, The Roots, has a clearer perspective than most Philadelphians his age.

"I've played the Capital, I've played the Apollo, I've been inside the Uptown Theater," said Thompson, who now serves as bandleader for the Emmy Award-winning "Late Night with Jimmy Fallon," and musical director for Philly's wildly popular "Welcome America!" concert that takes place on the steps of the Philadelphia Museum of Art every Fourth of July. "Technically, one of the very, very first Roots shows was sort of an audition. They had this contest/audition that they were holding at the Uptown Theater in like, 1989, that we went to.

"I definitely think it's a Philadelphia landmark, and I've been hearing talk of them trying to restore it and bring it back. I would personally like to be a part of that process, if possible. Whatever fundraising needs to be done and that type of thing, I would like to see that through.

"I've actually talked to a lot of artists," Thompson said in regard to the theater. "My favorite, I'd say, was the last time I talked to Teddy Pendergrass. I got to rap to him in the studio like about 2004, and he was like, 'Yeah, man! I used to always see your father at the Uptown Theater!' Teddy was really graphic in his description. He was like, 'Yeah, man! You don't understand! We'd come here at like 12:00 in the afternoon, they'd show a 'Three Stooges' cartoon. You'd get in for 50 cents. A box of popcorn would be 15 cents. You'd sit in the balcony and then a comedian would come on and maybe a magician, and then they'd have like a female Go-Go dancer on next, and then you could see some groups perform . . . basically, all day!' That's the tradition, and that's the tradition that I think we're missing today."

Another young warrior that was influenced by the late, great soul singer, Teddy Pendergrass, is Charles "Charlie Mack" Alston. The physically imposing six-foot-nine enforcer, who once served as a bodyguard for Will Smith and "Jazzy" Jeff Townes, is best known for his annual "Party 4 Peace Celebrity Weekend," and as a successful producer, promoter, entrepreneur and fearless community activist. Alston has proven time and again that he is capable of getting things done in the City of Brotherly Love and recognizes the Uptown's value to its overall landscape.

When I spoke to him in 2010, he, like Dantzler and Questlove, expressed his willingness to help revitalize the venue.

"Teddy told me some stuff about the Uptown Theater," said Alston, who actually produced a biopic on Pendergrass, starring soul singer/actor Tyrese Gibson. "That's the only person I've really had that conversation with about the Uptown Theater, but I'll tell you one thing. That particular area, what I'd love to have happen, is I would love to create Harlem. That's would I would love to do. I think that it's needed, I think that it would be received well.

"Look at Harlem. How many jobs are up there? It's a lot of people making a lot of money, and it's beautiful. We allow ourselves to be treated a certain way. We don't have to be treated in a certain way. We can get together and pool our resources together, and we can do that here. That's would I would love to have happen. Not that I gamble, but I think I'm gonna play that Power Ball and see if I can hit it! I'm not a gambling man, but I'm just sayin'. I need an influx of cash in a major, major way, 'cause I would do it! I'm tellin' you! I would turn this city upside down! They'd be like, 'Wow!'"

As young lions such as Dantzler, Thompson and Alston look toward the future of the Uptown, veteran entertainers can look back and fondly remember how the theater shaped their careers, and to a certain extent, their lives.

"Places like [the Uptown] need to be preserved, just like the Apollo," said Mavis Staples. "They tore the Regal Theatre down. I got so mad girl, when they let them tear that Regal Theatre down! These are keepsakes! People like Lena Horne, Redd Foxx—all these people were on that stage! Billie Holiday . . . Just think about this generation—what they would think of the Uptown Theater if they knew what happened up in there?"

"What made it so good with the Apollo, the Regal and the Uptown was that you had seven days to really meet and enjoy your peers—the guys you had heard all these years and did maybe one show or a concert, but not really getting to know 'em,' said Blue Lovett. "That was the opportunity to meet Poogie and all the guys we knew about, but really didn't know. We got a chance to meet and deal with them on an everyday basis. It was really nice. Nona and Patti and all of them . . . we sat down and played cards and we just got to know each other between shows. You didn't have that much time because it was so back to back to back, but it was great. That was our going to college."

In regard to the young generation that has yet to "discover" the Uptown, Nona Hendryx added, "One of the things the theater did was it inspired their grandparents to produce their parents, who produced them! So they should revere that place, and do all they can to help rebuild it, because it's a part of their legacy. The music that grew out of Philadelphia, to the point of Gamble & Huff, starting with Dee Dee Sharp and 'Mashed Potatoes.' That whole Philadelphia scene—Dick Clark, 'Bandstand,' Jerry Blavat—the Geator with the Heater, Philadelphia was really important to music. And for quite a few years, if you go back to the teenage heartthrobs like Frankie Avalon—all of the Bobby Soxers that came out of that place, and Georgie Woods was a major influence as well, in early rock and roll and R&B. So a lot of the music that they have today came about as a result of a home like the Uptown Theater for all the artists who came and played there.

"It also brought business to the community—to the neighborhood, because artists stayed in the hotels, they ate in the restaurants, they bought clothes there. It helped the community, so having it there again could only help the community as well." The iconic Kenny Gamble agreed and said, "If the Uptown was put back in shape, all those businesses would thrive."

"We want to make sure people understand that the preservation of the Uptown Theater is vitally important," said Richardson. "Besides it being something that celebrated the heyday of rhythm & blues, it also has some architectural value, and we want to preserve the architectural value."

Now that the restoration of the Uptown has actually begun, there is cause for optimism. In April 2012, after a 32-year hiatus and a $29 million renovation, the Howard Theatre, which closed in 1980, had its grand reopening.

That the Howard has been successfully transformed into a viable entertainment entity bodes well for the possibility of the Uptown returning to its rightful place in the historical and cultural fabric of Philadelphia.

While restoring the Uptown will be a monumental task, my hope for the future is not only that a new generation of talented artists will perform on that hallowed stage, but that extraordinary veteran entertainers like Jerry Butler, Patti LaBelle, Blue Lovett, Gerald Alston, Smokey Robinson, Nona Hendryx, Sarah Dash, Mavis Staples, Eddie Levert and Walter Williams, who are so much a part of the Uptown's history, will return to the place that is so dear to their hearts.

It would be great to see contemporary soul singers such as Ne-Yo, Jaheim, Tyrese, Tank, Mario, Avant, Musiq Soulchild, and maybe even Bobby Brown, if he promised to be on his best behavior, battling on the Uptown stage along with talented ladies like Jazmine Sullivan, Ledisi, Heather Headley and Estelle. The Uptown could provide an intimate atmosphere for the mellow music of Kem, Dwele, Anthony Hamilton and Brian McKnight, as well as a perfect home base for The Roots, and once the parking issue has been addressed (Personally, I would seek Temple University's cooperation in that area), hometown humorists Bill Cosby and Kevin Hart could do one—and two—night engagements there.

History has shown that the Uptown is a perfect venue for comedy and could be a prime location for Philly's exciting jazz scene, particularly in light of the fact that most big name jazz artists that come to the area are booked outside of the city at the Keswick Theatre in Glenside, Pa. Finally, the return of Amateur Night could once again uncover bright young artists whose voices have yet to be heard.

The Uptown Theatre was a beacon of pride, hope and strength for Black Philadelphia. Not only was it a technologically superior venue where gifted musicians like Sam Reed, Jimmy Heath, Thom Bell, Wilmer Wise and Earl Young could lay the foundation for long noteworthy careers, the Uptown was a sanctuary where inner city kids could build a lifetime of sweet memories as they watched some of the most talented entertainers on the planet work hard, create magical moments and strive for excellence.

It was a place where a young boy like Kevin Eubanks could be inspired to become a world-class musician, and a kid who literally lived right around the corner could become a star, if only for a moment.

The Uptown Theatre made it possible for Miss Pearl, an ordinary neighbor lady with extraordinary cooking skills, to become a successful entrepreneur, and was a haven where someone who was different, like the lovable Moo Moo, could earn a living, make friends and finally feel as if he belonged.

The historic venue allowed a young man with a dream and the passion to pursue it to "wiggle" his way into the music business, and ultimately, into the Rock and Roll Hall of Fame.

Finally, the Uptown Theater, a major source of gainful employment for dozens of willing workers in the community, was the springboard for a vibrant new sound, as well as a place where the powerful and charismatic

Georgie Woods could make or break careers, calm social unrest and inspire an entire generation of artists and audiences alike.

"The Uptown was a magnet," Kenny Gamble said in conclusion. "That's what we became. Philadelphia International Records became a magnet for artists to record and be a part of that sound that we had created."

---

[1] United States Department of the Interior—Heritage Conservation and Recreation Service
[2] United States Department of the Interior—Heritage Conservation and Recreation Service
[3] www.apollotheater.org
[4] Broadcast Pioneers of Philadelphia

ACKNOWLEDGEMENTS

THE UPTOWN THEATER'S place in my own life made researching and writing "Joy Ride! The Stars and Stories of Philly's Famous Uptown Theater" a labor of love, and with great appreciation I'd like to recognize the entertainers, artisans, experts and entities that assisted in the completion of my first book.

First and foremost, I thank God for preparing me for this intriguing odyssey, and my mother, Mary L. Roberts, who has devoted her life to her family. Mom, your love, strength, fire and spirit have made me who I am today.

I am grateful to have had the opportunity to interview broadcast legend Georgie Woods on several occasions before his passing, and hear the exciting and provocative story of the Uptown phenomenon directly from the man who made it all possible.

I would also like to acknowledge and thank Kenny Gamble, whose career was so profoundly influenced by his own experiences at the Uptown, for contributing the foreword to "Joy Ride!", for all of his encouragement, for his insight into the development of The Sound of Philadelphia, and for confirming my belief that "we need to tell our own stories."

To Sam Reed, I truly could not have written this book without you! Thank you for sharing your outrageous anecdotes and personal mementos with me, and for your patience with my never-ending questions!

To my "Magnificent Seven," the mighty musicians of the Uptown Theater—Sam Reed, Leon Mitchell, Earl Young, Thom Bell, Odean Pope, Wilmer Wise and Jimmy Heath—you supremely talented gentlemen are the very foundation of this book. Thank you for trusting me with your precious memories!

I would also like to express my deepest gratitude to Nancy Goldman, who made it possible for architect Henry Magaziner to share such valuable information on the Uptown before he passed away, and to Joseph Shemtov of the Free Library of Philadelphia's Rare Books Department, who located and accessed some of the rare artifacts from the Uptown that are included in this volume.

I cannot say enough about my brilliant colleagues Abdul R. Sulayman (photography) Calvin Rankin (art & design), Sirage Yassin (Information Technology) and Patrick Doherty (proofreading), who allowed me to rely on their technical skills and expertise during the production of "Joy Ride!" as well as my fellow authors, Donald Hunt, Anthony Davis and Diane Denard, for providing the road map for my incredible journey.

To Weldon McDougal IV (a.k.a. "Pudgie"), thanks again for your extreme generosity in letting me share your father's priceless pictures with the world, and to these extraordinary entertainers of the Uptown Theater, thanks not only for sharing your memories with me, but for defining an unforgettable era in Philadelphia history:

Jerry Butler, Leon Huff, Patti LaBelle, Sarah Dash, Nona Hendryx, Mavis Staples, Eddie Levert, Walter Williams, Otis Williams, Marlon Jackson, Bootsy Collins, George Clinton, Spike Lee, Bill Cosby, Blue Lovett, William "Poogie" Hart, the late Al Goodman, Fred Wesley, Maceo Parker, Smokey Robinson, Jerome "Little Anthony" Gourdine, Phil Terry, Robert "Big Sonny" Edwards, Barbara Mason, Dee Dee Sharp, Chubby Checker, Russell Thompkins, John Oates, Kevin Eubanks, Fatin Dantzler, Bob Angelucci, Ahmir "?uestlove" Thompson, the late Joe "Butterball" Tamburro, Carl Helm, Charles "Charlie Mack" Alston, Gilda Woods and Linda Richardson, as well as the Philadelphia Clef Club of Jazz & the Performing Arts.

Finally, to the late music pioneer Weldon A. McDougal III, our time together was much too brief, but the knowledge that you passed on to me, your startling stories and your striking vintage photos will serve to perpetuate the legend and the legacy of Philly's famous Uptown Theater.

SPECIAL THANKS

MY HEARTFELT THANKS to legendary Philadelphia drummer Earl Young, the extraordinarily gifted entertainer that inspired me to write this book, and whose music continues to bring so much joy to so many people around the world. Earl, I thank you for your guidance, which has never failed me, and for sharing your incredible experiences with me—both good and bad. You have led by example and have been right beside me for every step of this fascinating journey. As I've written in so many of my articles over the years, you truly are the heartbeat of The Sound of Philadelphia, and as promised, your own compelling and captivating story will be next. No one deserves it more. Believe in the magic!

Edwards Brothers Malloy
Thorofare, NJ USA
April 30, 2013